Cacti &
Succulents
NORTH & SOUTH, INDOORS & OUT
BY WILLIAM C. MULLIGAN

GROSSET
GOOD LIFE
BOOKS

PUBLISHERS • GROSSET & DUNLAP • NEW YORK

Acknowledgments

Cover photograph by Elvin McDonald

The author expresses his appreciation to the following for permission to use their illustrations in this book: Abbey Garden: p. 7 left, p. 10 top right, p. 14 right, p. 24 bottom right, p. 25 top, p. 26 top, p. 29, p. 31 bottom, p. 32 top, p. 62 top, p. 62 bottom left, p. 62 bottom right, p. 55 top right, p. 55 bottom right, p. 73 bottom right, p. 74 left, p. 74 bottom right, p. 75 bottom, p. 75 top left, p. 75 top right, p. 76 bottom right, p. 76 top right; Molly Adams: p. 39; Ralph Bailey: p. 41 top left, p. 45 top left; Phil Fein: p. 14 top left; Fernwood Plants: p. 74 top right; Howard Graf: p. 12 right, p. 13 bottom right, p. 44 top right; Grigsby Cactus Gardens: p. 32 bottom, p. 33 top, p. 33 bottom, p. 51 bottom left, p. 51 top right, p. 53 top right, p. 54 bottom right, p. 54 top right, p. 56 bottom right, p. 56 middle right, p. 56 top right, p. 73 top left, p. 73 bottom left, p. 73 top right, p. 76 top left; Jeannette Grossman: p. 43 top; Henrietta's Nursery, p. 50 bottom right, p. 50 bottom left, p. 50 top right, p. 50 top left, p. 51 bottom right, p. 51 top left, p. 52 bottom left, p. 52 bottom right, p. 52 top left, p. 52 top right, p. 53 bottom left, p. 53 top left, p. 54 top left, p. 54 bottom left, p. 55 left, p. 56 top left, p. 76 bottom left; Hort-Pix: p. 7 top right, p. 7 bottom right, p. 8 bottom, p. 9 top left, p. 9 top right, p. 9 bottom left, p. 9 bottom right, p. 10 bottom right, p. 10 top left, p. 11 top right, p. 11 bottom right, p. 13 top left, p. 13 top right, p. 14 bottom left, p. 23 left, p. 24 left, p. 24 top right, p. 25 bottom, p. 28, p. 30 left, p. 37 bottom, p. 38 top right, p. 38 bottom right, p. 40 top right, p. 41 top right, p. 41 bottom, p. 43 bottom, p. 44 left, p. 44 bottom right, p. 45 top right, p. 45 bottom, p. 46, p. 49 top, p. 49 bottom, p. 53 bottom right, p. 59 top, p. 61 top, p. 61 bottom, p. 63 top, p. 63 bottom, p. 64, p. 65 bottom; The Howland Associates: p. 11 left, p. 48; Jackson & Perkins Company: p. 26 bottom; Peter Kalberkamp: p. 67, p. 68; Ward Linton: p. 8 top, p. 30 bottom right, p. 37 top right, p. 56 bottom left; Frank Lusk: p. 18, p. 19, p. 20; Elvin McDonald: p. 13 bottom left, p. 30 top right, p. 31 top, p. 37 top left, p. 59 bottom, p. 60 top, p. 60 bottom; George W. Park Seed Co., Inc.: p. 23 right; Maynard L. Parker Modern Photography: p. 10 bottom left, p. 12 top left, p. 34, p. 40 left, p. 40 bottom right, p. 42; Ezra Stoller Associates: p. 65 top; Ed Sievers: p. 12 bottom left; Max Tatch: p. 38 left; U.S. Forest Service: p. 36; U.S. Soil Conservation Service: p. 6.

Contents

1
The Most Unusual Family of the Plant Kingdom

Cacti and the other succulents represent an incredible diversity of plants—from miniatures to giants, leafless to leafy, cuddly soft to impossibly thorny. Often the subject of erroneous myths, these unusual plants are viewed with apprehension by many growers, but they're actually easy to care for and make strikingly beautiful plantings both indoors and out.

Cacti and succulent grower/hobbyists are sometimes considered a strange breed, not only because the objects of their affection are so bizarre and mysterious but because these people are so enthusiastic in their praise of the water-retaining desert and tropical dwellers and cultivate them lovingly, often to the exclusion of all other plant forms.

Cacti and succulent growers certainly are not strange, but they are definitely attuned to the universal in plants. Shrewdly, they are aware of the challenge and enjoyment of being a part of nature's mysterious ways.

As the plant craze sweeps the country and gains momentum, more and more people are discovering that they favor certain plants or plant families and are concentrating their efforts on those; ferns, bromeliads, begonias, African violets—each has its own fans and fan club. But no group offers as much plant versatility and variety or deserves a larger host of fans than the cacti and succulents.

What Are Cacti and Succulents?

Succulents are plants that are capable of storing large amounts of water over a long period of time. As the earth evolved and atmospheric changes took place, scarcity of water in many areas caused these plants to adapt themselves cleverly; leaves evaporate water easily, so they became smaller or disappeared altogether—as in the case of cacti—and the stems either became the whole plant or took over from the leaves, to a great degree, the job of water retention and photosynthesis.

All cacti are succulents but not all succulents are cacti. Succulents comprise selected plants from many different families—the amaryllis, daisy, milkweed, and lily, among others. The *Cactaceae* family, of which all cacti are members, is, by the water-retaining nature of its plants, included in the group categorized as succulents. In other words, all plants called cacti are members of one botanical family, but the group of plants referred to as succulents is comprised of water-retaining plants from various families. Some non-cactus succulents such as the columnar euphorbias may look like cacti, but the true cactus has specific characteristics that distinguish it from look-alikes. On close examination one of the most evident is the formation of areoles. Cactus plants are dotted with these little soft protuberances from which sprout the spines, flowers, and new growth. Some of the euphorbias are covered with similar spines, but you'll see that they are not cacti if you look closely—the spines are not borne from areoles.

The conception of many that all cacti are spunky desert dwellers that bravely endure scorching sun and heat is not entirely correct. Some are epiphytes (air plants) that live in trees in the world's tropical jungles. Not as hard-pressed to retain moisture as their desert relatives, these cacti are less fleshy and have more leaf-like growth.

By far the greatest variety in form is found among the desert cacti. From large columns or candelabra shapes to the tiniest of spheres, these plants have devised all kinds of ingenious ways to overcome their environment. The ball shape of some cacti is one of nature's cleverest designs; it combines the greatest volume for water retention with the least amount of plant surface for evaporation. And the ribs of many cacti enable them to expand and contract accordion-fashion, as they swell when water is available and shrink when it isn't. The spines (some stiff and sharp, others as long and soft as hair) of cacti are a means of protection, not only from predators but also from the scorching desert heat, much the same as an animal's skin is kept at an even temperature with the help of its fur coat.

Climate and Locale

Just as you might ask a new acquaintance, "Where do you come from?" it's important to know the native habitats of the cacti or succulents you wish to add to your household. If you duplicate or at least closely approximate the conditions of their home environments, your plants will be comfortable and healthy.

All cacti are indigenous to the Western Hemisphere, but many have escaped to other parts of the world. Surprisingly, some grow in the cold climates of Canada and southern Chile. Most, however, are found in the desert regions of the United States and Mexico and in the warm areas of the West Indies and Central and South America.

The other succulents can be found just

Giant Saguaro cacti (Carnegiea gigantea) *rise as high as 30 feet—huge sentinels in the bleakness of their desert surroundings near Tucson, Arizona.*

about anywhere in the world. Their great diversity includes plants suited to every known climate and locale. They grow in the rain forests, deserts, plains, and mountains of the Americas (*Agave, Echeveria, Euphorbia*), Asia (*Sansevieria, Sempervivum*), and Africa (*Aloe, Cotyledon, Crassula*).

Something for Everyone

Transform an outdoor garden into a desert or tropical landscape, or create miniature succulent and cactus landscapes indoors with dish gardens and container plants. Whatever, you'll soon discover the rewards of growing these

The great diversity of cactus and succulent plant forms are displayed in this western garden exhibit at a fair.

Mammillaria pseudocrucigera. *Some of the most beautiful of all blooming plants, even among those cultivated, are the desert cacti.*

fascinating plants. Though many look as though they're about to say, "Take me to your leader," they never cease to be interesting in the way they grow, and in their striking shapes, foliage and coloring. And when you least expect it, a prickly little cactus may give birth to a spectacular bloom. Cactus flowers are especially vivid in color, and one bloom will often outsize the plant from which it bursts forth.

Our most popular Christmas plant, the poinsettia (*Euphorbia pulcherrima*), is a succulent that will grow well indoors or outdoors

A cereus cactus specimen plant—living sculpture that commands admiration.

Aloe arborescens *(candelabra aloe) in flower in its tropical habitat.*

Agave americana *'Marginata' is a sizable native of Mexico and the southwestern United States. Both aloe and agave are available in smaller varieties suitable for home containers.*

in temperate areas. Although precise amounts of light and dark are required for it to bloom again (the brilliant red "flowers" are actually leaf bracts—the yellow centers are the real blooms), a potted poinsettia gift plant makes a handsome and welcome year-round foliage plant.

Another plant of the Euphorbia family that's a splendid container candidate is the crown-of-thorns (*Euphorbia splendens*). It has brown thorny stems and bright red or coral-colored flowers.

Other succulents among the many that make attractive houseplants are the stylish agaves (of the Amaryllis family) and aloes (of the Lily family), both with long, tapering leaves that radiate from the plants' centers. Especially interesting is the partridge-breast aloe (*Aloe variegata*) that bears red and yellow bell-shaped flowers.

The Crassula family offers an endless variety of unusual yet attractive succulents. Among these are: *Sempervivum tectorum* var. *calcareum*, artichoke-shaped rosettes that are suited for container growing indoors or as rock-garden or border plants outdoors. The burro's tail (*Sedum morganianum*), with clusters of red flowers and trailing growth that can reach lengths of up to five feet, makes an ideal hanging-basket plant. The pen-wiper plant (*Kalanchoe marmorata*) has beautiful bluish-gray leaves flecked with maroon. White flowers bloom at the end of a long stem that rises up from the plant's cluster of thick leaves. The true jade plant (*Crassula argentea*) is an especially pleasing yet easily cultivated container choice. It survives too much or too little sun or water, grows very fast, and bears racemes of pale pink flowers.

Of the Lily family, the oxtongue (*Gasteria maculata*), as its name implies, has thick, tongue-shaped leaves that are dark green with white flecks. Long, narrow stems produce little hanging red flowers. Another member of the Lily family, the fairy washboard (*Haworthia limifolia*), has leaves similar in shape to the oxtongue but crossed with a series of ridges, hence the plant's name. Hanging, bell-shaped flowers are green outside and white inside.

Among the interesting succulents of the

The branching growth of a jade plant (Crassula argentae) *(above) and* Echeveria glanca *rosettes (below) complement each other in this strawberry jar planter.*

The velvet leaf Kalanchoe beharensis *is one of many attractive plants of the many kalanchoe species.*

Milkweed family are string of hearts (*Cero-pegia woodii*) and hairy starfish flower (*Sta-pelia hirsuta*). String of hearts makes a fine hanging plant, with its long, trailing stems that bear heart-shaped, mottled leaves and unusual black flowers. The hairy starfish flower grows clumps of cactus-like stems, but its most distinctive feature is described by its name; its large, star-shaped blooms are hairy on the inside and maroon in color.

The thick, tongue-shaped leaves of Haworthia linifolia *resemble those of gasteria, aloe, and other unusual members of the Lily family.*

Stapelia flowers look so like starfish that they have been given that name. Their slight odor of carrion attracts blowflies for pollination in the wild.

A seashore planting of succulents.

Lithops bella, *a split rock in bloom.*

The Mesembryanthemum (*Aizoaceae*) family contains probably the most unusual of succulents. Many sit on the soil surface and appear to be nothing more than smooth, egg-shaped rocks. Species of the genus *Lithops* look like rocks that have been split; each has a cleft separating what are actually two very thick, somewhat globe-shaped leaves. Bright yellow flowers grow out of the cleft. Tiger jaws (*Faucaria tigrina*) has white-speckled, tooth-edged leaves and large yellow flowers. The faucarias include almost forty species, all fitting this general description.

Other families, some of whose members are unusual and attractive succulents, are Geranium, Portulaca, Grape and wandering Jew.

Yuccas *(foreground) and sedum ground cover, both hardy, thrive in full sun in a northern garden.*

Knobby tiger jaws (Faucaria tuberculosa) *is one of the many faucarias that grow in this interesting pattern.*

Ideally Suited to Today's Oft-Absent or Vacationing Gardeners

Living with greenery is an increasingly popular trend; more and more people are recognizing the warmth and decorative beauty of plants and the enjoyment of tending them. And while many of us are filling and surrounding our houses with growing things, we don't always have as much time as we would like to devote to their care. Cacti and succulents are the answer to this dilemma; they make handsome and unusual additions to any environment, yet require relatively little upkeep.

An unusual outdoor container planting of hardy echeveria and sedum that can be brought indoors when weather turns too cold or wet in winter.

Yuccas withstand frost and in summer shoot up stalks with showy blooms every other year. Only the yucca moth can pollinate this plant.

Give most cacti and succulents plenty of sun outdoors, in a greenhouse, or on a window sill indoors and you don't have to worry about much else. They can adapt to low levels of humidity and need only minimal amounts of water. Pests are seldom a problem because the skin of these plants is just too tough to be inviting.

Cacti and succulents are ideal plants for a weekend house at the seashore or in the country. At relatively low temperatures, they can be left in a sunny window and will require watering only about once a month. And the faster growing succulents will so change their

A dramatic effect is achieved with an arrangement of stone slabs planted with various succulents.

A raised bed is attractive and provides needed drainage for cacti and succulents.

Containers of tender succulents may be brought indoors easily with the onset of cold weather to provide an inside garden in a sunny window or glassed-in area.

shapes that your being absent part of the time will add to the enjoyment of growing them.

The versatility of cacti and succulents is excellently suited to today's trends in outdoor gardens. In areas of the country that are subject to frost, containers of cacti and succulents can be placed in the ground in imaginative arrangements, and brought inside in winter, which is the normal dormancy period for these plants.

Cobweb hen-and-chicks (Sempervivum arach-noideum) make a handsome winter hardy ground cover.

Some cactus genera—*Opuntia, Pediocactus*, and some species of *Echinocereus*—can withstand frost and may be left outdoors all winter. In spring and early summer these will reward you with large, breathtaking blooms.

If you're fortunate enough to enjoy the frost-free environments of Florida and the southwestern United States, then there is an almost infinite variety of cacti and succulents from which to choose to ornament your outdoor garden. Plant a lawn of blooming ice plants (of the *Aizoaceae* family) for a blanket of color, or such flowering plants as *Echeveria, Sedum,* or *Sempervivum*. For a desert garden of dramatic shapes, combine pin-cushion plants (*Mammillaria*) with columnar (*Cleistocactus hyalacanthus*) and golden-barrel (*Echinocactus grusonii*) cacti.

Ocotillo (Fouquieria splendens) *(left) and opuntia provide two starkly contrasting shapes among the great variety of succulent plants.*

Ice plant (Lampranthus emarginatus) *is covered with purplish-red blooms but makes a handsome ground cover of gray leaves in frost-free climes, even when not in bloom.*

This furry-looking columnar cactus (Cleistocactus) *will enhance a southern garden, either in this striking arrangement or grouped with barrel and other columnar cacti.*

Sedums and sempervivums in a dry wall planting. Provided with plenty of sun, these are hardy in northern areas and provide accents for flagstone steps and around trees.

Winter-hardy **Sedum** *spectabile* *makes an unusual, imposing flowering border set off against a carpet of trailing sedum.*

Flowers in Abundance

Cactus flowers are unequaled in the plant world for sheer size and brilliant color. The whites, yellows, purples, and reds that provide relief from the browns and greens of the desert can also be vivid accents in your garden. Many cacti will not bloom until reaching an advanced age and need lots of sun and heat to do so.

Coryphantha borwigii *and its related species such as lobevia, and those of rebulea, gymnocalyciume, and notocactus bear spectacular blooms on small plants.*

Orchid cacti (Epiphyllum x hybridus) *display showy blooms, some fragrant, in colors ranging from red and pink to yellow and white.*

Some will flower when young and even in containers indoors. Rebutias, for example, will often bear 2- to 3-inch blooms, sometimes on as small as a 1-inch plant, completely covering it with a mass of bright color.

No discussion of cactus blooms is complete without mention of the Christmas cactus (*Schlumbergera bridgesii* and hybrids). These are branch-type cacti that grow link fashion, with showy white or red flowers at the ends of the "branches." The flowers bloom around Christmastime in a profusion of color.

For the ultimate in exotic blooms, try one of the night-blooming cacti (species of *Cereus, Hylocereus, Epiphyllum, Monvillea,* and *Selenicereus*). These are similar in growth habit to the Christmas cactus, but the blooms are larger and truly spectacular. Opening only after dark and closing before dawn, they're heavily scented and often reach as much as 12 inches in diameter.

The orchid cactus (species of *Epiphyllum*), as its name suggests, represents another group of attractive bloomers. These are of the tree-dwelling, epiphytic variety which require more water than the desert types but have adapted themselves to survive drought conditions, and won't suffer if the drought happens to be your vacation trip. Some orchid cactus are night bloomers and others are day bloomers, depending on the species, and colors range from white, cream, and amber to lavender, purple, and red.

Among succulents other than cacti, colorful blooms are offered by the agaves, aloes, hoyas, and ice plants.

The abundance of choice is obvious, and success with all of these—whether flowering or not—is easier than you think if you take time to consider each plant's native habitat and the degrees of sun and moisture and the kind of soil it enjoys there. Your selection is limited only by the conditions you can provide in and around your own home. Don't expect the impossible, be attentive to any signs of distress or deterioration among your plants and you will become a successful cactus and succulent grower.

2
Caring for Desert and Jungle Dwellers

Beyond a few basic cultural requirements, cacti and succulents need minimal attention. Even if you forget to water them for a period, their moisture-retaining ability will keep them hale and hearty. And while most other plants need high humidity, cacti and succulents prefer the lower levels (10 to 20 percent) of the average home. However, considerations of soil and light described below are of the utmost importance. And we must be aware of and allow for the once-a-year period of dormancy characteristic of many of these plants.

Tender Care for Newcomers

When moved to a new environment, plants of any kind need time to adjust; they may require anywhere from ten days to two weeks to adapt to the conditions of your home and will demand greater care during this period than any time thereafter.

Whether your newly purchased plants arrive boxed from a mail-order house or in mint condition from a local nursery, try not to do anything that will add to the shock they have already suffered in transit, with one exception. A soft, sometimes mushy rot may appear on a newly arrived plant, a sign of overwatering. Don't throw it out. Cut out the rot with a clean razor blade, let the wound dry for several days. All will be well. Keep new plants in partial shade for a few days and water moderately. Then place them in a sunny window or, if you prefer, under lights (see page 30). But don't put them among plants you already have unless you are sure the newcomers are free of pests and disease. Even plants from the most reliable of nurseries may be pest-ridden, so before you contaminate your entire plant collection take the precaution of immersing your new plants in water for a few hours almost to the rim of their containers. If there are any pests in the soil, they'll come to the surface in short order.

If you receive a new plant unpotted (bare root), root it in the ground outdoors or indoors in a container of soil as soon as possible. Don't water for a few days unless the plant appears especially dry or shriveled, in which case you might moisten the ground or potting soil sparingly.

Container Culture

Soil: Contrary to popular belief, cacti and succulents will not grow in pure sand. They need the nutrients and moisture-retaining capability provided by a mix of ingredients. A good, basic mixture for cacti and succulents consists of equal parts garden loam, sand, and leaf mold, but keep in mind that the most effective mix for healthy growth depends on the climate conditions of your locale. In warm weather areas a light, well-drained mixture is best, and in cooler areas where less watering is required, a heavier soil is more suitable.

To make desert cacti feel more at home, add extra sand and some gravel to the basic mix; for jungle dwellers such as rhipsalis and epiphyllum, the preferred mix is one part osmunda or fir bark to one part garden loam. For the health of your plants a potting mix should provide good drainage combined with moisture retention, so be sure to mix all ingredients thoroughly to insure a loose, friable texture.

Commercial mixes available at your local nursery or garden center are thoroughly blended and sterilized against pests and bacteria. Unless these prepared soils are combined specifically for cacti and succulents (such packaged mixes are available), a little doctoring may be necessary. Many experienced growers have had great success with commercial mixes to which they add a small amount of vermiculite and sand for drainage, and a few tablespoons (to a 6-inch pot) of manure and bone meal for added nutrients. The bagged soil-less mixes perform well and are becoming increasingly popular for houseplants, but they contain no nutrients. Use them only if you are prepared to follow a steady and time-consuming feeding program.

Light: Most cacti and succulents require direct sun during some part of the day for successful flowering and optimum growth. If this isn't possible, don't give up the ship. These plants are remarkably adaptable, and although they may not grow quickly or bloom often, if at all, they will survive in indirect light or partial shade. Rebutia and lobivia cacti respond better than most to these less-than-ideal conditions.

Potted plants should be turned periodically to provide even light on all sides of the foliage, but not if the plant is about to bloom. Any change in light at that time may cause the flower buds to drop.

Of the succulents other than cactus, almost all do best in direct sunlight. Members of the Mesembryanthemum family, especially, thrive in the desert conditions of full sun and little water. Exceptions among the succulents are *Kalanchoe blossfeldiana* and *K. pumila*, which grow best in partial shade.

As an indication of the amount of light your plants are getting, it's helpful to know that foliage cacti and succulents respond to sufficient light with deeply colored foliage, while the absence of optimum light causes the foliage to grow pale or less vibrantly colored.

Moisture: This area of plant culture is the one that inspires the greatest lack of assurance among growers, especially novices. It's the kind of thing for which there are no hard, fast rules, but with experience and genuine attentiveness to your plants, you'll develop almost a second sense regarding their watering needs.

In general, the desert-dwelling cacti require less moisture than the other succulents. Another rule that can be applied generally is never water either type on cold or overcast days, because these conditions coupled with excess moisture promote the growth of fungi. Also, plants in large pots do not need as frequent watering as those in smaller pots; a 4-inch pot will use up all of its moisture in a day, while a 10-inch pot will take a week to dry out. Another general rule: When plants are sprouting new growth, give them plenty of water, but hold back during their period of dormancy.

With each watering, water thoroughly until drainage seeps from the bottom of the container. Don't water again until the soil has dried out.

Fertilizers: Unlike most other houseplants, cacti and succulents, under ordinary conditions, do not require frequent feeding. They will achieve acceptable growth without fertilizer, one exception being older, specimen plants in large containers. Because these grow more slowly, they don't need frequent repotting; they must be fed regularly, preferably during spring and summer, however.

For any plant to survive, it must have: potassium for good stem growth and flowering and seed production; nitrogen for healthy leaves and new growth; and phosphorus for proper development toward maturity. Although cacti and succulents extract most of what they need of these from their potting mixes, I would recommend a moderate feeding program as an insurance factor, especially if you have the time or if you are not likely to repot your plants frequently.

Add a little bone meal once a year (1 teaspoon to a 6-inch pot), or apply a weak solution once a month of 10-5-5 fertilizer (numbers refer to the ratios, successively, of nitrogen, potassium, and phosphorus present in the formula). Feed these to your plants only during the spring and summer months, which is their active growing period.

Potting and Repotting: Cacti and succulents will grow well in almost any kind of container as long as it's of the proper size and has holes in the bottom for the drainage of excess water. The standard terra-cotta pot is the old standby of experienced growers because it provides good drainage, comes in an assortment of sizes, and is relatively inexpensive. But if you have a penchant for decorative containers without drainage holes, simply plant in a terra-cotta pot and drop it inside whatever decorative container you've chosen. After watering, be sure to empty the outer container of any water that has drained from the clay pot.

Container size is a very important consideration. If too small, there will not be enough soil to provide the plant with adequate nutrients, and if too large, the soil will hold more moisture than the plant can absorb, increasing the likelihood of rot. Follow these rules of thumb: A ball-shaped cactus should be planted in a pot with a rim that is 2 inches wider than the diameter of the plant; a columnar cactus should be provided with a pot that has a rim diameter measuring half the height of the plant. In both cases, the pot should be deeper than it is wide.

Before planting, always scrub old or new pots with hot, soapy water to remove dirt and possible insect eggs. Rinse well and then submerge them in water overnight so they'll be completely waterlogged and will not absorb moisture from the soil.

For the actual planting, first place shards of clay (break an old pot into small pieces) at the

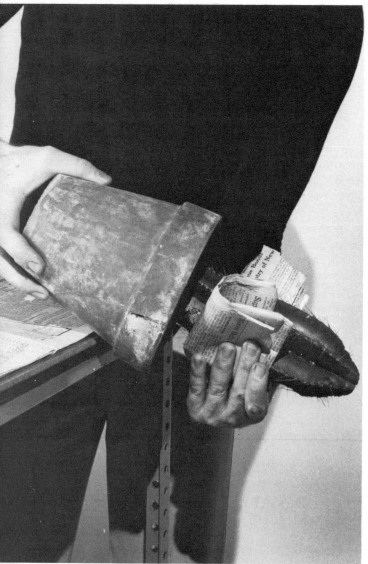

For safe removal of cactus and soil-root mass from pot, tap the pot on table edge while holding cactus with several thicknesses of newspaper.

bottom of the container to insure drainage. Cover these with a thin layer of sphagnum or peat moss. This will keep the soil from filtering down into the pieces of clay. Add about 2 inches of potting mix, and then set the plant in it. Add or remove soil, as needed, until the plant is at the proper height. Then pour the remaining soil around the plant. To keep your fingers free of sharp spines, shape a piece of paper like a chute, place some soil in it, and then tilt the "chute" so the soil slides into the container. For those cacti and succulents that are especially sensitive to moisture, substitute a thin layer of attractive gravel for the very top layer of soil. This will keep the plant from coming into contact with excessive moisture and adds an exotic touch.

Wait at least several days before watering a newly potted plant, so that any damaged roots will not rot and will have time to heal.

A welcome dividend of cacti and succulents is that they grow relatively slowly, necessitating much less frequent repotting than other plants. Those in 4- to 7-inch containers will require repotting no more than every two years, and those in larger containers can go three years before needing to be repotted. Spring and fall are the best times to repot, but if this isn't possible or if your plants are in desperate need of repotting, you will do no harm giving a plant a new container during summer or winter.

Remove a plant from its old container by inverting it and tapping the pot rim edge sharply against the edge of a counter or table-top. During this operation, you can hold a prickly plant with a double thickness of newspaper. When the plant and soil mass are free of the container, pour in the last of the soil with a paper chute and tamp it down with a narrow stick. For easy and safe handling of a spiny cactus while removing soil from its roots and placing it in the new container, roll up a piece of newspaper and flatten it into a long, narrow strip; wrap this around the cactus and join the ends to form a handle. For smaller cacti, substitute scissor-type kitchen tongs for the newspaper. Like porcupine quills, cactus spines will detach themselves and remain in your fingers. They also will penetrate gloves;

the tongs and newspaper are the only ways to handle cacti safely.

Rest and Recuperation: Like hibernating bears, most cacti and succulents need a once-a-year period of rest (varying from a few weeks to several months), when growth ceases and both moisture and nutrient needs lessen. This occurs during the winter months for most cacti and some succulents, and at other periods of the year and for varying lengths of

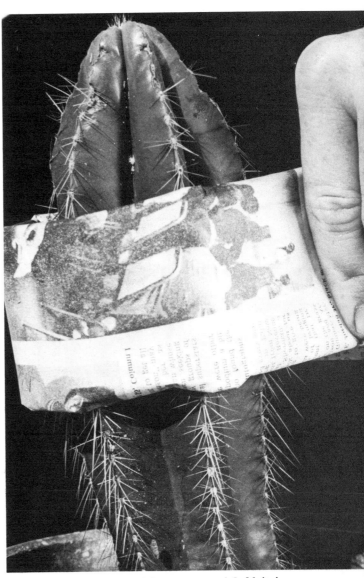

To plant in new pot, position cactus and hold it in place with a "handle" fashioned from rolled-up newspaper.

time for the remaining succulents. Exceptions are kalanchoes, aloes, and agaves, which have no readily discernible periods of dormancy.

During their resting time, your plants will need cooler temperatures at night (around 55°F.) and only enough water to keep them from shriveling. A sort of perked-up look and fresh new growth is the signal that your plants have awakened. When this occurs, they'll need more heat and normal watering.

New Research: The science of plant cultivation is not always as exact as researchers and growers would like it to be. Plants are living organisms, and like people, their well-being is subject to an almost infinite number of variables. Medical researchers are constantly discovering more effective ways to care for the human organism, and horticultural researchers, although on a smaller scale, are finding new and better ways to cultivate plants.

You're probably familiar with the study being done in the area of extrasensory perception as it applies to plants. The essence of the theory is that plants react to human brain waves or thought processes. This may be great news for those people who are tired of talking to their plants; they need do no more than encourage them with good, positive thoughts. A book called *The Secret Life of Plants* by Peter Tompkins and Christopher Bird is a provocative and comprehensive report of the experiments being done in this field.

Cacti and succulents are not exempt from experimentation, and growers are making some startling discoveries that refute the traditional and generally accepted rules. One of these growers, Michael Tifford, has had success treating cacti and succulents much the same as other plants. The following is from an article by Elvin McDonald that appeared in the August 1974 issue of *House Beautiful.*

Tifford, a wholesale grower of bedding and house plants on Long Island, began to grow cacti from seeds. Originally, he followed the established rules, but both sprouting and growth were disappointing. Reasoning that almost anything would be an improvement, Tifford began to experiment. He first tried treating the cactus seeds and seedlings as if they were ordinary bedding plants or vegetables—say petunias and tomatoes—or the ferns like the holly-leaf or the Boston.

His greenhouses have an atmosphere of fresh, moist air, no steam bath, mind you, but

To keep fingers away from spines, form a single sheet of paper into a chute to add soil around a newly potted cactus.

no sauna either. In the fall and winter seasons, all the glass and plastic coverings are cleaned to admit maximum light, but some shading is added from early spring until the late summer.

Probably most important, however, is moisture in the soil. Tifford uses a growing medium that is both humusy and gritty and he keeps it uniformly moist. There is, of course, a distinct difference in the meaning of the words "moist" and "wet." Tifford's rule is that a cactus or other succulent watered in the morning should be only moist or approaching dryness by nightfall. It should not be allowed to remain wet overnight. In other words, right *compares to a moist sponge from which you cannot squeeze any water;* wrong *is a wet sponge that yields a trickle of water. Tifford has found that when any cactus is too hot and too dry, it goes dormant, the same as in the desert.*

Tifford's revolutionary treatment of cacti has produced phenomenal results. Year-old seedlings are four times the usual size and healthier than plants grown in the traditional manner. Older plants flower much more freely.

Outdoor Culture

If you live in Southern California, Florida, or the southwestern states where climate conditions are ideal, you can transform your outdoor garden into an eye-catching panorama of cacti and succulents with little effort or continuing care. These plants will survive the severest of droughts, and their varied and striking shapes will remain to enhance your environment.

In areas of frost, you can surmount the problem by planting only winter hardy species (see Chapter 4), or by taking advantage of the portability of containers. These can be sunk into the ground or grouped imaginatively on or around patios or terraces, and brought inside during the winter.

The most important things to remember about cultivating cacti and succulents outdoors are: They must be provided with plenty of sun and they must be planted so that excess moisture can drain readily. Choose absolutely unshaded areas of your garden and plant on a slope or in a raised bed. If you do select a level site, dig the planting holes about 2 feet deep and refill with a sandy, gritty mix in place of the original soil. To protect winter hardy plants during frost, cover the immediately surrounding soil surface with a layer of cocoa mulch, leaves, or bark chips. In both frost and frost-free areas, water lightly during the summer and not at all during the fall and winter. These pest-free plants require no garden sprays, if given proper culture.

3
Cacti/Succulents in the House

Deciding which cacti and other succulents to begin a collection with is no easy matter; in fact, it can be downright mind-boggling when you consider the thousands of possibilities. After you have read this book and studied the pictures, you will have some idea of the selection available. It's also a good idea to visit one of the major public displays of cacti and other succulents, (for addresses, see Appendixes). You can also send away for the catalogs and listings of specialists who ship by mail (also see Appendixes).

Just in case all of this research leaves you even more bewildered and undecided as to which cacti and other succulents are most likely to perform well as houseplants, I have prepared a listing of the kinds that do well for me in a New York City apartment, or that have been recommended by other authors and friends whose judgment I respect.

The small dimestore plants are varied and some grow quite slowly. Six or eight of them of different heights and colors in a single glass or ceramic bowl will last for several years. Changing in shape constantly, they produce young knobs and projections that fall off and take root when inserted between the stones or into the colored sand that covers the soil. If there is no drainage, water sparsely or the roots will rot. With drainage, it isn't necessary to dampen more often than every week or two.

Planters or groups of larger pots arranged on cork (to protect the floor) in the corner of a glass-walled room create a desertlike garden to offset a cold winter. Or a sunny windowsill completely encased by a shallow pan and covered with sedums and sempervivums brought in in the fall absorbs the winter sun.

Cacti should be planted or grouped together for best effect and the same with succulents, but there are exceptions for those with an artistic eye. And in these days of large interior plants, nothing is more striking than a single columnar specimen of almost ceiling height, or a special table with large striking cacti or succulents of suitable kind or shape.

Recently, many apartment dwellers have added gro-light fluorescent units to their indoor gardens. As winters progress, a sunny window may lose hours of bright light, and many a loved plant has hung sadly or grown spindly, or dropped leaves like snowflakes. Many fluorescent light manufacturers are still experimenting with growth, blooming, and distance of light from plant. Among the most successful plants under light are the cacti/succulents which need the long hours of light but also flourish in the dry air of central heating. You can have your desert or jungle and apartment, too.

Astrophytum asterias (sand dollar) can grow to an attention-getting size.

Best Houseplant Cacti/Succulents

Latin Name	*Popular Name*
Adromischus cooperi	plover eggs
A. maculatus	calico hearts
Aeonium canariense	giant velvet rose
A. tabulaeforme	green platters
Agave victoriae-reginae	queen agave
Aloe striata	coral aloe
A. variegata	partridge breast; tiger aloe
Aporocactus flagelliformis	rat-tail cactus
Ariocarpus fissuratus	Mexican living rock
Astrophytum asterias	sand dollar
A. nyriostigma	bishop's cap
Beaucarnea	
Cephalocereus senilis	old man
Cereus peruvianus monstrosus	curiosity plant
Ceropegia woodii	string of hearts
Cleistocactus straussi	silver torch
Coryphantha elephantidens	elephant tooth cactus
Cotyledon barbeyi	hoary navelwort
Crassula argentea	jade plant
C. cultrata	propeller plant
C. deltoidea	silver beads
C. perforata	necklace vine
C. perfossa	string o' buttons
C. pseudolycopodiodes	princess pine

A Collection of Container Cacti.
1. Echinocactus grusonii *(golden barrel)*.
2. Haagocereus bicolor.
3. Cephalocereus nobilis.
4. Cleistocactus straussii.
5. Cephalocereus chrysacanthus.
6. Echinocactus grusonii *(golden barrel)*.
7. Nyctocereus serpentinus cristatus *(snake cactus)*.
8. Mammillaria geminispina.
9. Coryphantha.
10. Machaerocereus eruca *(creeping devil)*.
11. Melocactus.
12. Mammillaria prolifera.
13. Mammillaria geminispina.
14. Coryphantha.
15. Notocactus haselbergii.

Best Houseplant Cacti/Succulents

Latin Name	Popular Name
C. rupestris	rosary vine
C. teres	rattlesnake tail
C. tetragona	miniature pine tree
C. tricolor jade	tricolored jade
Echeveria derenbergii	painted lady
E. elegans	Mexican snowball
E. pulvinata	chenille plant
Echinocactus grusonii	golden barrel
E. horizonthalonius	eagle claws
Echinocereus sasayacanthus	rainbow cactus
Echinocereus	hedgehog cactus
Echinopsis multiplex	Easter-lily cactus
Espostoa lanata	Peruvian old man

Gymnocalycium mihanovichii friedrichii *(rose-plaid cactus).*

Euphorbia lactea cristata *(elkhorn or brain plant) is one of the most statuesque and variable succulents for the house and summer garden.*

Hoya carnosa variegata *(wax plant) is one of the many trailing hoya hybrids that form clusters of star-shaped fragrant flowers.*

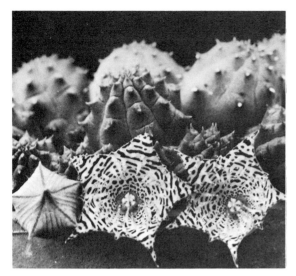

Huernia kennedyana.

Best Houseplant Cacti/Succulents

Latin Name	Popular Name
Euphorbia caput-medusae	Medusa's head
E. fulgens	scarlet plume
E. heterophylla	mole plant
E. lactea cristata	elkhorn; brain plant
E. mammillaris	corncob cactus
E. mammillaris 'variegata'	Indian corncob
E. pulcherrima	poinsettia
E. splendens	crown of thorns
E. tirucalli	pencil tree; milk bush
Faucaria tigrina	tiger jaws
Furcraea gigantea	giant false agave
F. selloa marginata	variegated false agave
x Gasterhaworthia *	royal highness

* x indicates hybrid.

The tiny brilliant scarlet blossoms, like drops of blood, of the crown of thorns (Euphorbia splendens) are probably the reason for the popular name.

Best Houseplant Cacti/Succulents

Latin Name	Popular Name
Gasteria verrucosa	oxtongue; pencil leaf
x Gastrolea beguinii *	pearl aloe; lizard tail
Gymnocalycium leeanum	yellow chin-cactus
G. mihanovichii	plain chin-cactus
G. mihanovichii friedrichii	rose-plaid cactus; red cap
Haworthia	
Hoya carnosa	wax plant
Huernia	
Kalanchoe beharensis	velvet leaf; elephant ear
K. pinnata	air plant; miracle leaf
K. tomentosa	panda plant
Lemaireocereus marginatus	organ pipe
Leuchtenbergia principis	prism cactus; agave cactus
Lobivia	cob cacti
Mammillaria bocasana	powder puff
M. camptotricha	birdsnest
M. candida	snowball pincushion
M. elongata	golden stars
M. fragilis	thimble cactus
M. hahniana	old lady cactus
M. lasiacantha	lace-spine cactus
M. plumosa	feather cactus
Myrtillocactus	branching candelabra cacti
Nopalea	tall, almost treelike plants
Notocactus submammulosus	lemon ball
N. rutilans	pink ball cactus
N. scopa	silver ball
Nyctocereus serpentinus	(cristate) snake cactus
Opuntia basilaris	beaver tail
O. bigelovii	cholla cactus; teddy bear
O. clavarioides	black fingers
O. cylindrica	emerald idol
O. dillenii	tuna
O. erectoclada	dominoes
O. erinacea	grizzly bear
O. fulgida mamillata monstrosa	boxing glove
O. microdasys	bunny ears
O. microdasys albata	angora bunny ears
O. microdasys albispina	polka dots
O. microdasys 'Lutea'	honey Mike
O. oricola	prickly pear
O. rufida	cinnamon cactus
O. schickendantzii	lion's tongue
O. streptacantha	tuna cardona
O. strobiliformis	spruce cones

* x indicates hybrid.

Notocactus submammulosus.

Sedum autumn joy is a glorified form of Sedum spectabile *with 6-inch pinkish flowers spreading 30 inches wide and 30 inches tall. It is hardy.*

Best Houseplant Cacti/Succulents

Latin Name	Popular Name
O. turpinii (glomerata)	paperspine cactus
O. vulgaris (moncantha)	Irish mittens
O. vulgaris variegata	Joseph's coat
Oreocereus celsianus	old man of the Andes
O. fossulatus	mountain cereus
Pachypodium	can be dwarf or treelike
x Pachyveria haagei *	jewel plant
x P. scheideckericristata *	jeweled crown
Parodia maassii	Tom Thumb cactus
Portulacaria afra variegata	elephant bush
P. afra variegata tricolor	rainbow bush
Rebutia	tiny specimen called crown cactus
Rhipsalis cassutha	mistletoe cactus
R. warmingiana	popcorn cactus
Sansevieria guineensis	bowstring hemp
S. trifasciata	snake plant
S. trifasciata 'hahnii'	birdsnest
Schlumbergera bridgesii	Christmas cactus
S. gaertneri	Easter cactus
S. gaertneri makoyana	cat's whiskers
Sedum morganianum	burro tail
S. pachyphyllum	jelly beans
S. rubrotinctum	Christmas cheer
S. sieboldii	October plant
S. spectabile	autumn joy
S. treleasei	silver sedum
Stapelia hirsuta	starfish flower
S. variegata	star flower
Trichocereus	relatively large plant; a genus of organ pipe cacti
Zygocactus truncatus	Thanksgiving cactus

* x indicates hybrid.

Specimens as Sculpture

In recent years the general trend in houseplants has been away from small tabletop or window-sill specimens to ceiling-reaching trees and great cascading hanging baskets, often with medium-sized shrubs in between. The same is true of cacti and other succulents in particular. In fact, some of these are absolutely stunning as pieces of living sculpture. Uplight, downlight, or crosslight one of them and you will be amazed—and delighted—with the different effects possible.

Some of the best kinds from which to select a large, important specimen include:

Latin Name	Popular Name
Agave	
Aloe	
Astrophytum	sand dollar
Cephalocereus senilis	old man cactus
Cereus peruvianus monstrosus	curiosity plant
Cleistocactus	
Echinocactus grusonii	golden barrel
E. horizonthalonius	eagle claws
Euphorbia caput-medusae	Medusa's head
E. grandicornis	cowhorn
E. tirucalli	pencil tree; milk bush
Kalanchoe beharensis	velvet leaf
Lemaireocereus marginatus (Pachycereus)	organ pipe
Myrtillocactus	
Trichocereus	

Perhaps it is unnecessary to say, but nevertheless a word of caution: Be very careful in placing spiny or sharp-needled plants where you or any other person might walk into them. One shudders at what might happen from the careless placement of a large agave, for example, with its dagger-sharp leaf tips.

What about light for these large plants? And care? They are usually costly investments, and besides, one develops an attachment for these rather quickly; a casualty is not to be taken lightly. For one thing, be *sure* the plant you purchase is established in a container of

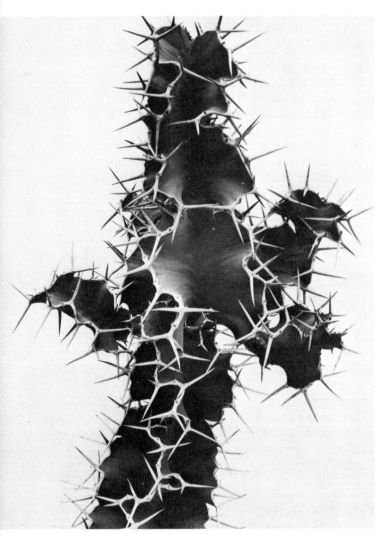

The interesting growth habit of Euphorbia grandi-
cornis *(cowhorn euphorbia) makes a dramatic
statement in any room setting.*

other approach to containerizing large cacti and other succulents is to grow them in a utilitarian container which has a drainage hole. Slip this inside a slightly larger decorative jardiniere, but be sure that water does not collect and stand in the base. If you place a waterproof saucer inside, woven baskets make great containers for specimen cacti and other succulents. Those with Indian design motifs seem especially appropriate.

For convenience it is a good idea to place the containers for large specimens on some kind of dolly. This provides instant portability so that you can wheel them around the house for a change in decorative effect, or to receive greater light. A dolly also facilitates an easy indoor-outdoor existence if that fits your scheme; in other words, you can wheel the specimen outdoors for real recuperation and growth in ideal light during warm dry weather, but well before frost is expected they can be rolled back inside.

The amount of sunlight received indoors in most houses and apartments is hardly sufficient even under the best of circumstances for long-range health of most cacti and other succulents. The use of supplementary artificial light is not only beneficial to the plants' health but the cosmetic effects are obviously desirable. Incandescent floodlights (General Electric's Cool Beam or Sylvania's Cool-Lux, for example) are the answer. These may be mounted in ceiling track systems, in uplight or downlight units, or in any stand-mounted socket. These floodlights should be used only in ceramic sockets. Spotlights are not suitable; they concentrate the light too much and may cause burned spots on cacti/succulents.

Floodlights of the type suggested are available in sizes ranging from 75 to 300 watts. These should be placed approximately 2 to 4 feet away from the plants. As the sole light source for a large specimen, it may be necessary to use two or three floodlights, perhaps of 150-watt size, burned 12 to 16 hours out of every 24. Plugging them into an automatic timer is more satisfactory than remembering to do the on-off work yourself—besides, who will provide days and nights if you go away for several days?

soil, that is to say, well rooted. It follows that the best investment will be a specimen that has been nursery-grown, not one recently ripped up and robbed from the desert.

A large clay pot with a drainage hole and a matching saucer makes the best container for a large specimen. Remember, however, that unglazed clay saucers seep some moisture through the bottom, enough to eventually spoil a fine wood floor or carpeting. You can avoid this problem by cutting a circle of cork to fit underneath the saucer; that little extra moisture will evaporate through the cork. The

If floodlights are used merely to supplement natural light, they may need to be burned for only six to eight hours in the evening when, incidentally, you will most enjoy the effects of dramatic lighting.

What to Grow If You Have No Sun

Best known for their tolerance of less than abundant sunlight are the succulents *Beaucarnea, Ceropegia, Hoya,* and *Sansevieria.* One grower friend of mine, Francesca Morris, who lives in a Westchester suburb north of New York City, has excellent success in north-facing windows with ceropegia, hoya, and sansevieria; she also keeps an epiphyllum in this same exposure in the wintertime. In his new book, soon to be published, *The Encyclopedia of House Plants,* Elvin McDonald also suggests the following cacti/succulents tolerant of less than perfect natural light indoors:

Rattlesnake tail (Crassula teres) *will grow with no direct sun, indoors or in a semi-shady spot in a southern garden.*

Latin Name	Popular Name
Acanthocereus pentagonus	big-needle vine
Acanthorhipsalis monacantha	spiny rhipsalis
Aeonium canariense	giant velvet rose
A. haworthii	pin-wheel
Aichryson	
Bowiea volubilis	climbing onion
Chiastophyllum	
Cissus quadrangularis	veld grape
C. rotundifolia	Arabian wax cissus
Clusia	
Crassula argentea	jade plant
C. cultrata	propeller plant
C. deltoidea	silver beads
C. perforata	necklace vine
C. perfossa	string o' buttons
C. pseudolycopodiodes	princess pine
C. rupestris	rosary vine
C. teres	rattlesnake (tail)
C. tetragona	miniature pine tree
Cryptocereus	
Deamia testudo	tortoise cactus
Disophyllum	
Epiphyllanthus	
Epiphyllopsis	
Epiphyllum x hybridus *	orchid cactus
Erythrorhipsalis	
Euphorbia tirucalli	pencil tree; milk bush
Gasteria caespitosa	pencil leaf
Hatiora salicornioides	drunkard's dream
Haworthia	
Heliocereus speciosus	sun cactus
Huernia	
Kalanchoe tomentosa	panda plant
Lepismium	
Leuchtenbergia principis	prism cactus
Monvillea	
Nopalxochia	
Opuntia vulgaris variegata	Joseph's coat
x *Pachyveria clavata cristata* *	
Pedilanthus tithymaloides	redbird cactus
Pereskia aculeata	lemon vine
P. grandifolia	rose cactus
Pfeiffera	
Portulacaria afra variegata	variegated elephant bush
Pseudorhipsalis	

* x indicates hybrid.

Latin Name	Popular Name
Rhipsalidopsis	
Rhipsalis cassutha	mistletoe cactus
R. warmingiana	popcorn cactus
Schlumbergera bridgesii	Christmas cactus
S. gaertneri	Easter cactus
S. gaertneri makoyana	cat's whiskers
Sedum morganianum	burro tail
Selenicereus grandiflorus	queen of the night
S. pteranthus	king of the night
S. urbanianus	nightblooming cereus
Senecio rowleyanus	
Weberocereus	
Zygocactus truncatus	Thanksgiving cactus; crab cactus

Christmas cactus (Schlumbergera bridgesii) *offers a continuous profusion of showy rose-red to orange-red flowers, in season.*

was reported by Henry F. Lee in the September 1974 issue of *Green Scene*, a magazine published by the Pennsylvania Horticultural Society. Dr. Lee recommends the use of Gro-Lux Wide-Spectrum tubes placed in standard reflector units and burned 16 hours out of every 24. For a growing area approximately 18 by 24 inches you will need a standard industrial fixture with either two or three 20-watt tubes; for an area 24 by 48 inches you will need a fixture with two or three 40-watt tubes. Replace the tubes at least once a year, preferably every six months, otherwise the light is

Burro tail (Sedum morganianum), *a handsome trailer in a well-chosen planter, will do well without a great deal of sun.*

The Fluorescent Way

If you have no natural light indoors sufficient to sustain healthy growth of cacti and other succulents, fluorescent light provides a ready substitute. It is, at this time, limited to the culture of seedlings, young plants, and kinds that remain fairly small at maturity—say no more than 8 to 10 inches tall.

Fluorescent-light culture of cacti/succulents is at present a fairly new idea. The most up-to-date experience of a successful home gardener

The beautiful flowerlike shape of the Dudleya candida *is emphasized by the light of the sun. When the plant is brought indoors in winter, an incandescent grow light can do the same for it.*

too dim for the best growth of your plants.

For recommended varieties to grow under fluorescent lights, study Dr. Lee's listings in the accompanying chart.

Cacti and succulents all grow and bloom faster under fluorescent lights because of the longer duration of light. Here a collection includes an old man cactus, a little partridge, aloe, and others.

Cephalocereus senilis, *the old man cactus, is a fuzzy white curiosity and a relatively friendly one; its long spines are somewhat stiff but safe to the touch.*

Selected List of Choice Plants Grown from Seed Under Lights

Cacti

Latin Name	Popular Name
Astrophytum asterias *	sand dollar
Astrophytum myriostigma	bishop's cap
Cephalocereus senilis	old man cactus
Cereus peruvianus monstrosus	curiosity plant
Cleistocactus straussi	silver torch
Dolichothele longimamma	finger-mound
Echinocereus * (many species; beautiful long-lasting flowers)	rainbow cactus
Ferocactus acanthodes	fire barrel
F. covillei	Coville's barrel
F. nobilis	
Gymnocalycium mihanovichii friedrichii *	rose-plaid cactus (one of the best bloomers)
Gymnocalycium * (several others)	chin-cactus spider cactus plain cactus prism cactus
Leuchtenbergia principis	
Lobivia * (several)	
Mammillaria bocasana *	powder puff
M. bombycina *	silken pincushion
M. elongata *	golden stars
M. geminispina (bicolor)	whitey
M. gulzowiana	
M. insularis *	
M. klissingiana	
M. longiflora *	
M. nivosa *	
M. pseudocrucigera	
M. pyrrhocephala *	
M. zuccariniana *	
Notocactus crassigibbus * (long-lasting flowers)	
N. haselbergii *	white-web ball
N. magnificus	
Parodia aureispina *	Tom Thumb
Setiechinopsis mirabilis *	

* *Successful flowering under lights.*

Other Succulents

Latin Name	Popular Name
Aloe (many species; mixed seed starts well in sphagnum)	
A. haworthia	
Argyroderma (several)	
Cheiridopsis (several)	victory plant
Dinteranthus puberulus * (germinate seeds in the dark)	
Faucaria * (many species)	tiger jaws
Hoodia gordoni	
Huernia * (many species)	
Lapidaria margaretae	karroo rose
Lithops * (many species)	stoneface cleft stone
Odontophorus *	
Schwantesia *	
Stapelia * (many species)	
Tavaresia grandiflora *	thimble flower
Titanopsis calcarea	limestone mimicry

* Successful flowering under lights.

Aloe haworthia, *perhaps the handsomest of the small aloes, with white spurs on dark green spiky leaves, can be grown from seed under lights.*

For the display of cacti and succulents in your home, there are no hard and fast rules concerning arranging and grouping. Try to achieve a distinctive effect by relying on your own sense and knowledge about the plants' natural habitats. Cacti often stand alone in the desert, and for that reason a single potted cactus lends an austere and dramatic focal point to any room setting.

Cacti and nonleafy succulents grouped in bowl or dish plantings or in individual containers will inevitably evoke the image of the desert. And if you like, you can further this effect with the addition of small rocks or pieces of sun-bleached wood or bone. Standard terra cotta containers or planters of rough-

Lapidaria margaretae, *a miniature (pot is 2 inches across) of the same family as ice plant, will form 2-inch yellow flowers.*

White-web ball (Notocactus haselbergii) *has brilliant red flowers that last a week and keep on budding for four to eight weeks.*

Miniature Lithops *(stonefaces) are no larger than 1 inch in diameter. Real stones are combined with succulents in this clever tray planting.*

hewn material will complement this likeness.

To recall the lushness of the tropical jungle, group epiphytes, cacti and leafy succulents together or along with appropriate nonsucculent plants such as orchids, dracaenas, bromeliads, and tall Kentia or Arica palms. Terra cotta containers that are molded in various shapes or woven baskets of all kinds work best in achieving the tropical look.

Above all, don't be afraid to be original or adventuresome. Experiment with the contrasts and similarities of totally unrelated plants. If you want to set ferns alongside cacti, no one could be displeased by the beautiful counterpoint of these two opposite ends of the plant spectrum.

This free-form pebble-finish concrete planter is filled with small, ground-hugging crassulas with the bold Crassula falcata *planted for accent.*

4
In the Garden

If you live in a mild climate where freezing temperatures seldom, if ever, occur, cacti and succulents in the outdoor landscape will not be strangers. However, in cold regions where winter temperatures below freezing are the rule, plant selection is more limited. In fact, the only common ones are found among the many prickly pears (*Opuntia species*), the sedums and sempervivums, and yuccas, but these are by no means the only ones. Many succulents evolved in cold regions. Note pages 36–45 for their hardy plants or look-alike substitutes.

The photographs in this chapter have been selected to show as wide a variety as possible of landscape uses of cacti and succulents. If the plants shown will not tolerate freezing temperatures, feasible look-alike cold-hardy substitutes are suggested in the captions. If there are none, you might consider wintering over selected plants in a frost-free place. In warm weather you can sink the pots to the rims in the outdoor landscape, adding a final mulch of pebbles or stone chips so that the plants will appear to be growing in the ground even though they are actually rooted in pots of soil.

Architecture is a matter of major concern when you are dealing with these desert and jungle plants. Spanish or stucco frame dwellings suggesting the south can be greatly enhanced with softening succulents of size or large doorside cacti of height, with rounded raised beds of smaller plants in place of antique cannas and such. Some northern perennials of similar shape and quiet tones, such as lupines, the dollarlike silver honesty and green and white calladium, can look appropriate at a distance.

For modern, straight-lined, rough wood exteriors or woven fences and the like, contrasting tones of both cacti and succulents, either in low beds or of some height, make a striking contemporary effect, either the leafy forms or bold shapes. Spiky northern plants—the cork-bark euonymus, the Harry Lauder bush (if you want) or irregular evergreens such as the Atlas cedar and distorted blue-gray spruce—can make a memorable setting for a home. Limestone facings and glass walls are remarkable settings whether the desert and jungle plants are on the inside or outside. Perhaps the greatest advances can now be made in creating tropical scenes in the northern outdoors. Or mix plantings without regard for city or climate. The challenge is here.

Some barrel cacti (Echinocactus wislizeni) shown in their natural setting. Garden plantings should *suggest elements of a plant's native habitat for best effect.*

Sempervivums, usually called hen-and-chicks, come in many sizes and colors. In cold weather most of them take on even more vivid coloration. In this planting they have been arranged to emphasize variations in size and color. White marble chip mulch completes the design.

This unusual hedge is a planting of Euphorbia candelabrum (candelabra cactus). These branch out into trees 30 feet high in their native desert.

In warm-climate gardens like this one, the variety of cacti/succulents from which to choose is practically unlimited. Here the sizes vary from the towering column of Carnegiea gigantea (left) to ground-carpeting types, and to the leafy green rosettes of yucca (right). The large barrel cactus (center) in this cultivated garden is the same species shown in the photograph on page 36. There are frost-tolerant forms of yucca and barrel cactus, but none for the carnegiea.

Agave victoriae-reginae *(queen agave) makes a handsome all-year accent plant for warm-climate gardens. Where frost occurs, a sempervivum may be used instead.*

This entryway planter features a carefully pruned pine tree with the leafy green rosettes of greenovia, a member of the Crassula family. In cold climates, hardy sempervivums might be used to give a similar effect.

Cryophytum crystallinum *is one of many so-called ice plants with daisylike flowers. This particular one is frost-sensitive.*

Sedum sieboldii *(October plant) makes a fine ground
cover in cold as well as warm climates. It may also
be planted in rockery and wall pockets where the
stems and leaves will cascade gracefully.*

A stylish arrangement of Kalanchoe beharensis *in serial containers easily brought indoors for the winter for a remarkable effect beside a glass wall.*

Aloe plicatilis, *with its precisely arranged, long, thick leaves and flowers, is the accent plant in this landscape vignette. Where freezing occurs in winter, this same aloe might be used in warm weather simply by growing it in a pot sunk into the soil in summer, then moving it indoors for the winter.*

Various young and small-growing cacti are used here with pebble mulch to create a garden of subtle textural contrast.

Low-growing crassulas, here in full bloom, carpet the ground around a handsome agave.

Crassula perfossa *is a stunning all-year ground cover in frost-free gardens. For cold climates it can be planted in a pot or hanging basket for wintering over inside.*

This narrow, slightly raised planter bed at the base of a stone wall is planted with two kinds of echeverias, the planting spaces for each divided by

narrow strips of redwood with a stone chip mulch adding the final artistic touch.

A shady flight of steps with both hardy and tender plants that can be "lifted" for the winter months: the step-risers are covered with creeping thyme (hardy); below the base rock—the lovely tender echeverias; to the left of the broad step—tender iceplant; and, just above, hardy hen-and-chicks. An aloe accent plant, above left, makes it all seem tropical.

The gray and wine-red rosettes of **Sedum** *spathulifolium 'Cape Blanco' are used here as a* *foil for rocks and pebbles in a Japanese-style garden. This sedum is hardy in northern gardens.*

This slightly raised planting bed in a warm-climate garden includes low rosettes of echeveria, slightly larger agave and crassula with columns of cephalocereus to the right. Where freezing occurs, *a similar effect might be achieved using sempervivums,* Sedum spectabile *and a hardy opuntia (for the tallest accent).*

Sempervivum arachnoideum, *the cobweb houseleek, covers this rocky bank, along with common green houseleek and a variety of interesting mosses and lichens. These sempervivums are quite able to withstand up-north winters.*

Fouquierias, the Ocotillos of the desert, rise like bizarre candelabra in this tiered planting. Stone mulch in contrasting colors further accents the stark quality of the design. Yucca in flower (right) is also used.

This landscape vignette offers a study in textural contrast—sizable jade plants are edged by the lacy gray foliage of dusty miller and the green of wild strawberry. The pebble mulch walkway offers further contrast with the brick surface surrounding.

Sedum dasyphyllum *makes a fine-textured all-year ground cover in cold as well as warm climates. In season it is covered by the starry flowers shown here. It also makes a fine hanging basket plant.*

Sedum spectabile *is completely cold-hardy. Although the foliage dies to the ground when frosted, when warm weather arrives in the spring it sends up fresh new growth from the roots. In late summer the plants become smothered in white or pink flowers.*

By cultivating a variety of succulents it is possible to create pattern gardens like this one. The plants include agave, aloe, echeveria, jade plant, pencil cactus and crassula.

In this warm-climate garden, succulents serve as a foundation planting. Most notable is the elephant-ear Kalanchoe beharensis *(left). A variety of echeverias, some of them in flower, carpet the ground.*

The graceful rosette of aloe adds a pleasant contrast in texture. A piece of driftwood is effectively silhouetted against the wall.

5
By Choice
Not Chance—Collecting

The variety of cacti and succulents available is truly fascinating, but it can also be bewildering. One way to comprehend this vast grouping is to consider basic types according to size, predominant color of the foliage, body or spines, and the flowering or growth habits. The photographs in this chapter have been selected with these basic types in mind. For every plant shown you will likely find several others that are similar. As a beginning collector you might, for example, choose one plant from each category, presuming of course that you can provide the space and suitable growing conditions. On the other hand, you may wish to collect plants within a single category, for even the look-alikes have distinct differences which provide endless fascination to the true collector. Spine formations, for example, may appear at a glance to be the same, but look again—perhaps using a magnifying glass—and you will discern infinite variety.

A few decades ago, our grandmothers covered every available sill and table with African violets, behind a sun-softening curtain to protect the foliage from burning. Today, many of us have our own plant craze, and none is more satisfying than cacti and succulents. Some genera—aloe, agave, opuntia and many others listed in this book—are so broad that a compulsive collector can easily turn to any one of them. Often, after a few years of seeking variety, one settles down to the expertise of collecting one genus, joining its society (see Appendixes) and visiting its shows, even taking tours with a master horticulturist to see for oneself the great collections.

This country provides a tropical and subtropical environment in Texas and Florida, where the variety can easily overwhelm the first-time visitor. To see the native Caribbean trees there, especially in bloom, or catch sight of a fifty-foot century plant standing alone in the scrub with its twenty-foot bloom is not to be forgotten. Nor is it perhaps so different from the obsession of setting aside a sunporch encased in glass with euphorbias in all their dozens of forms.

With more than two thousand species of the cactus family to choose from (all originating in the Americas) and several tens of thousands of succulent (winter-storing) plants from thirty families of plants all over the world . . . well, why not specialize in collecting? Nobody ever collected them all.

Yuccas used with no other succulents or cacti can add to a northern garden a quality of the desert, flowering early in the season.

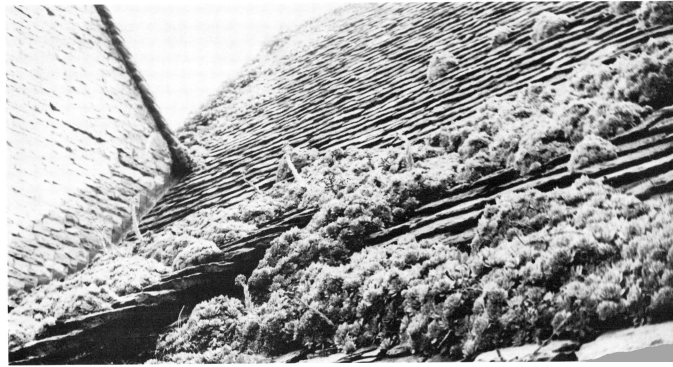

Roof garden? In Europe and New England, hardy sedum can be planted on a slate roof with no danger of introducing leaks. The effect is old-fashioned.

The north and the south meet in this western garden where the climate is cool enough for a grassy lawn. But hardy hen-and-chicks mix with tender aloes, and tall, hardy yuccas mix with tall, tender succulents.

Euphorbia lactea cristata.

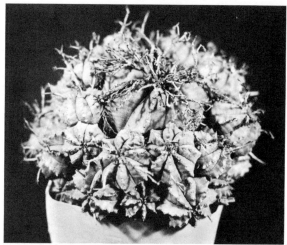

Euphorbia valida.

Euphorbia obesa.

Euphorbia hermentiana.

Astrophytum asterias.

Aeonium arboreum variegatum.

Coryphantha poselgeri.

Echinocereus knippelianus.

Frailea asterioides.

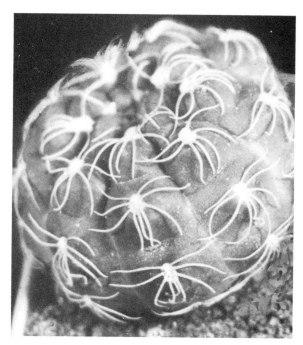

Gymnocalycium denudatum.

Mammillaria albicoma.

Horrida minor.

Lithops helmutii.

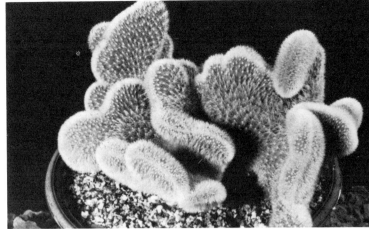

Hildewintera acriespina *crest*.

Mammillaria bombycina.

Kalanchoe pumila.

Neoporteria mammilloides.

Neobuxbaumia polylopha.

Notocactus rutilans.

Pachyphytum *'Blue Haze.'*

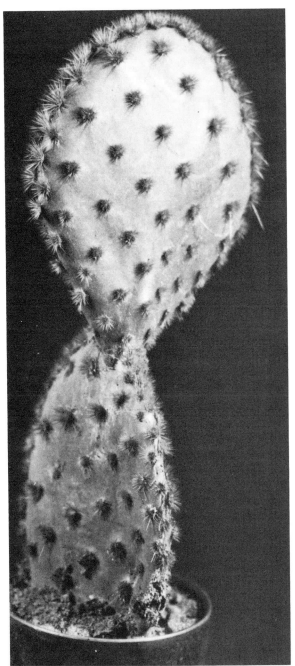

Opuntia acicularis.

Rebutia heliosa.

Sedum furfuraceum.

Oreocereus trollii.

Senecio scaposus.

Stenocactus multicostatus.

Tavaresia grandiflora.

Turbinicarpus schmiedickeanus.

6
Unusual Ways of Display

Part of the pleasure to be derived from growing a collection of cacti and other succulents lies in displaying them so as best to emphasize their natural beauty. Lighting effects are discussed in Chapter 3.

The trailers and creepers suggested for hanging baskets in the text which follows may also be cultivated in pots and displayed on a shelf or pedestal where the stems can cascade freely.

Cacti and Succulents for Hanging Baskets

Cacti and succulents are among the best of all plants for growing in hanging baskets. Indoors the main problem lies in providing them with sufficient direct sunlight, especially during the short and often dark days of late fall and winter. Otherwise they are uniquely suited to growing up in the air. One problem with most leafy basket plants is that when they are hung in the upper parts of a room—where they are most often desired for decorative effect—the temperatures up there are too hot in winter. And basket plants outdoors often suffer from drying out too frequently. The cacti and succulents included in the following list won't thrive if you are totally negligent about watering them, but, on the other hand, most of them won't suffer any great setback if the growing medium dries out occasionally for a few days.

Hanging basket containers you might use for cactus and succulents include:

- redwood boxes and cradles. Line these with polyethylene plastic (with drainage holes punched in the bottom) so that the growing medium does not all wash away between the slats; or you can line them with pieces of unmilled sphagnum moss or florists' sheet moss.
- wire or plastic hanging baskets (with open mesh construction). First line these with a thickness of unmilled sphagnum moss or florists' sheet moss; then add a liner of polyethylene plastic with holes punched in it for drainage.
- clay or plastic hanging pots. These are excellent, providing they have drainage holes. Cacti and succulents have a natural affinity for pottery, but not unless the container has provision for drainage. This is a rule you

might get by with breaking indoors where you control the amount of moisture, but not outdoors where rainfall reaches the containers.

After you have selected a hanging basket and lined it appropriately, fill with your favorite growing medium for cacti and succulents and proceed with planting. Some growers report success with the new soil-less mixes in hanging baskets, partly because these mixes are very lightweight and thus provide a more easily managed and mobile planting. With any soil-less mix—Jiffy Mix, RediEarth, or Supersoil, for example—it is necessary to feed a little with every watering while the plants are in active growth. A "little" means feeding at one-fourth to one-fifth the strength recommended for normal feeding. For example, if the directions say "one teaspoon fertilizer to one quart water," you would reduce the amount to one-fourth teaspoon fertilizer to one quart water.

Aloe ciliaris: Climbing aloe. Firecracker aloe. Hanging basket. May be used as a ground cover in frost-free climates. Spikes of red flowers in season.

Aporocactus: species and varieties. Rat-tail or whip cactus. Sprawlers and spreaders, excellent for hanging baskets. Flowers may be crimson, pink, or old rose. Likes sun and warmth. Occasionally seen trained upward on a wire or wooden trellis, espalier-fashion.

Bowiea volubilis: Climbing or sea onion. Twining, graceful, even bizarre stems grow upward from a green bulb that sits partially out of the soil. In time these stems develop a cascade effect. Will survive in a bright north window but prefers at least morning or afternoon sun indoors. May be cultivated as a curious—if not beautiful—hanging-basket specimen, or trained upward on a light trellis.

Ceropegia: species. Rosary vine. Hearts entangled. Long, dangling, wiry stems set with heart-shaped or small, slender leaves. Some are plain green, others marked in a silver mosaic. The strange, intricately formed flowers are truly fascinating if you examine them closely. Great hanging-basket plants indoors or out-

doors. As houseplants the ceropegias have an amazing tolerance for varying light levels, from that of a north window to a sunny southern exposure.

Echeveria: Belonging to the Crassula family, the range of these many-colored plants runs to the hundreds of species. Rosette shapes dominate, and the waxy white rosettes are surely the most appealing.

Epiphyllum: species and varieties. Orchid cactus (see illustration, page 14). Many recent hybrids have been bred specifically for growing in hanging baskets. Essentially they need shade from hot summer sun but plenty of direct sun the rest of the year. Plant in sandy but humus-rich potting soil. Feed and water freely in the summer; give no fertilizer in winter and water only enough to keep the stems from shriveling. The spring and summer flowers are spectacular, but well-grown plants are attractive in any season. Closely allied *Aporophyllum, Chiapsia nelsoni, Disapora,* and *Disophyllum* require similar care and make excellent basket specimens.

Harrisia: Night-blooming cereus (one of many so-called). May be grown as a large hanging-basket plant in a spacious sunny window in warmth.

Hoya: species and varieties. Wax plant (see illustration, page 24). Sometimes classified as succulents and often seen in the company of cacti and other succulents. These make beautiful hanging-basket plants. The foliage—which may be plain green; green-flecked with silver; or a combination of green, creamy white, and rosy pink or burgundy—is always attractive. In season the clusters of star-shaped flowers are exquisite—and fragrant.

Kalanchoe: Two species, *K. scandens* and the better-known *K. uniflora* (kitchingia), may be used as basket plants. *K. uniflora,* from Madagascar, makes a fine houseplant in a sunny window. Dangling lantern flowers of dark rose appear in the spring.

Kleinia: species. Several of these are satisfying to grow in hanging baskets. They include *K. heereianus* (gooseberry kleinia), *K. pendula* (inchworm plant), *K. radicans*, and *K. tomentosa*. In the house they need as much sun as you can give them.

Mesembryanthemum: Ice plant (see illustration, page 13). Both of these names are applied to a variety of creeper, trailers, and sprawlers that make attractive hanging baskets. As houseplants, all need a generous measure of sun. Specific names include: *Aptenia cordifolia variegata, Carpobrotus edulis* (Hottentot fig), *C. chilensis* (sea fig), *C. acinaciformis, Cephalophyllum alstoni, C. spongiosum, C. tricolor, Cryophytum crystallinum, Delosperma echinatum, Dorotheanthus bellidiformis* (Livingstone daisy), *Hymenocyclus croceus, H. herrei, H. purpureocroceus, Lampranthus multiradiatus* (sun rose), *L. emarginatus* and *Oscularia deltoides*. All are characterized by fairly small succulent leaves and an abundance of brilliantly colored daisy-like flowers.

Othonna crassifolia: Pickle plant. Drooping stems set with succulent leaves like miniature cucumber pickles. The flowers are half-inch yellow daisies. Provide an abundance of sun all year, plenty of water in summer but on the dry side in winter. An excellent and fairly easily obtained hanging-basket plant.

Peperomia: species. This popular houseplant is succulent-like, and certain kinds make splendid hanging baskets. Peperomias are touchy about water—too much or too little and they have a habit of turning up their toes, collapsing of rot at the base of the stems, and dying. Yet they are mostly carefree, easily cultivated plants in the light of an east, south, or west window. Best for hanging baskets are these species: *P. cubensis, P. fosteri, P. glabella, P. obtusifolia, P. prostrata, P. quadrangularis, P. scandens,* and *P. trinervis*. Houseplant baskets of these will summer well outdoors in partial shade, hanging from the branches of a tree, for example.

*In a heavy ceramic pot, with pockets in the sides like a strawberry barrel, a single genus—*Echeveria *(see page 58)—has been planted. Most echeverias are of the rosette form. In fair weather, this one is hung from the bough of a tree in the garden.*

The hybrid Disophyllum *on delicate white stems sends out its fragile white blossoms.*

Peperomia columella *is an ideal hanging plant. When the young upright stalks begin to hang down naturally, the pot can be suspended in a basket.*

The mistletoe cactus—Rhipsalis cassutha—has several look-alikes which are not pendant enough for a hanging basket such as the pencil tree.

Portulaca grandiflora: hybrids. Rose moss. This old-fashioned annual, most often seen carpeting dry, sun-baked areas in the garden, makes a superb hanging-basket plant outdoors in the summer. Plant seeds or set out started plants in baskets as soon as danger of frost has passed in the spring. You may expect flowers eight or nine weeks later—and then until fall frost. The best of today's hybrids have double flowers nearly three inches across. They are available in mixtures or in separate colors—all of which are spectacular.

Rhipsalis: Mistletoe cactus. These are mostly spineless with strange, slender, cylindrical branches, many of them with the unusual habit of shooting off new branches at acute angles. Grow in a mixture of fir-bark, sand, peat moss, and garden loam; water freely except not so much in the winter. Protect from hot, midday sun. Excellent houseplant hanging baskets, especially if you can provide a little better than average humidity in the winter. These look especially attractive in the company of stark, contemporary furnishings. The related and similar *Hatiora salicornioides* (drunkard's dream) and *Pseudorhipsalis macrantha* are equally fine basket plants.

Sansevieria parva: This succulent member of the Lily family has the fascinating habit of sending down long runners to two feet with baby plants on the tip of each. Like the common snake plant, in whose family it belongs, *S. parva* has a truly cast-iron disposition; hot or cool, moist or dry, sun or shade, it makes a striking basket plant when well grown and groomed.

Sedum: Live forever. This genus is rich in creepers and danglers suited to all kinds of airborne plantings. Mostly they are popular and widely distributed. Consider: *S. acre, S. dasyphyllum, S. lineare variegatum* (especially fine as a houseplant), *S. mexicanum, S. morganianum* (the choice burro or donkey tail sedum), *S. palmeri, S. sieboldi,* and *S. stahli* (coral beads or Boston bean). Of all, *S. morganianum* is surely the choicest; it is, in fact, a favorite among *all* hanging-basket plants. When you want to purchase the burro's tail sedum, growers inevitably will show you a fine old specimen with which they will not part, but then you'll have the pleasure of seeing your young (and relatively inexpensive) rooted cutting grow into an equally fine specimen. Outdoors, *S. morganianum* is best given protection from strong winds and stormy rains; otherwise many of the leaves will be broken off the stems.

Senecio rowleyanus: This strange succulent, with many African relatives, has creeping branches and berry-shaped leaves that distinguish it from the others.

Stapelia: Starfish flower. Carrion flower. These succulents with leafless, knobby stems have only one fault—and that lasts for a fairly brief time: The flowers smell of carrion. There are many different kinds; favored as a houseplant hanging basket is *S. variegata* whose fantastically marked flowers give off less of the offensive odor than some of the larger ones. Indoors it needs direct sun in an east, south, or west window. Easily cultivated.

Zygocactus: Thanksgiving, Christmas (see illustration, page 30) and Easter cacti. This grouping also includes *Rhipsalidopsis rosea,* *Schlumbergera bridgesii, S. gaertneri* (sometimes called a rhipsalidopsis), and *S. russelliana.* Besides these species there are dozens of new hybrids available today, many of which flower more freely. All bloom when days are naturally short; you'll upset their timetable if you allow artificial light to reach them at any time between sundown and sunup in the fall months. During these short days it is important to keep them on the cool side (preferably not over 65°F.), to water less and not to feed at all. All of these prefer a humus-rich potting soil, the same as you might use for begonias or African violets. They make excellent hanging-basket plants, preferably in a window that receives some direct sun in the winter months. While these jungle cacti do well in the dappled shade of a tree outdoors in summer, as houseplants they really do require some direct sun in order to grow well.

Green jade (Echeveria agavoides) *produces the larger leaves and trailing sedum produces the smaller ones in this wire basket.*

A remarkable sight, a round jug with round openings festooned with Senecio rowleyanus, *or a string of pearls.*

Bursera fagaroides, *in a Japanese bonsai planter, captures the illusion of an actual ancient miniature tree.*

Cacti/Succulents as Bonsai

Many fine specimens of hundreds of different cacti and other succulents take on the appearance of aged bonsai—miniaturized trees—when they are planted in traditional bonsai containers. Larger, older specimens may require the root room of a fairly deep, bowl-shaped bonsai dish. Smaller and young plants may be established in more shallow bonsai trays.

Some of the best plants for giving the instant effect of bonsai are:

Latin Name	Popular Name
Agave victoriae-reginae	queen agave
Anacampseros rhodesica	
Bursera fagaroides	
B. hindsiana	
B. odorata	
Euphorbia nivulia	
Fouquieria fasciculata	
Jatropha berlandieri	
Opuntia ramosissima	
Pachycormus discolor	
Plumeria acutifolia	West Indian jasmine; temple tree
Trichodiadema densum	miniature desert rose

The crown of the Trichodiadema densum, *known as the miniature desert rose, must be heavily pruned over a long period to achieve this effect of foliage and centuries-old trunk.*

Euphorbia nivulia, *one of the forms of this genus with normal-looking leaves, also in a Japanese bonsai planter.*

While the plants in the preceding list are fairly rare, there are two more suited to bonsai training which are popular and widely distributed: *Crassula argentea* (jade plant) and *Portulacaria afra* and *P. afra variegata* (elephant bush). After a few years of cultivating these with the roots cramped in small quarters, they begin to develop aged, enlarged, gnarled stems and smaller leaves in keeping with a bonsai.

Bowl and Dish Gardens

One of the most pleasurable ways to enjoy a collection of small cacti and other succulents is to combine them in a miniature desertscape which can be planted in any container that seems appropriate to the size, texture, and color of the plants. You can use pottery, plastic, clay pot saucers, bonsai dishes and trays, even clear Plexiglas. Since these containers have no provision for drainage, it will be necessary to first add a layer of gravel, followed by a layer of charcoal chips, then the final layer of your favorite planting medium for cacti and other succulents.

Before you actually begin planting, it is a good idea to sketch the dimensions of your container on a sheet of newspaper. Then arrange the plants within this area while they are still individually potted. You can try all kinds of spacing and different combinations until the effect is exactly what you have in mind. Use this as your planting scheme, removing one plant at a time, unpotting and repositioning it in the desertscape container. To assist in handling spiny plants, take a sheet of newspaper and fold it over and over into an inch-wide strip; wrap this around the spiny body and clasp together with your fingers. This makes a fine holder that will not damage the plant, and the spines will not wind up in your fingers.

Water bowl and dish gardens of cacti and other succulents very carefully. In the beginning the medium should be moist, but not too. If you can imagine potting soil as being wet, nicely moist, barely moist, or nearly dry, then try to keep your desertscape within the range between barely moist and nearly dry.

As the finishing touch for a desertscape,

A great fashion is the garden under a glass dining table. The Trumans introduced this at the White House.

Little Joshua trees is the name given to this collection of Sedum multiceps *dwarfed by a specimen stone.*

Easiest Cacti/Succulents for Bowl and Dish Gardens

Latin Name	Popular Name
Adromischus	plover eggs
A. maculatus	calico hearts
Aloe variegata	partridge breast; tiger aloe
Astrophytum asterias	sand dollar
A. myriostigma	bishop's cap
Cotyledon	
Crassula argentea	jade plant
C. cultrata	propeller plant
C. deltoidea	silver beads
C. perforata	necklace vine
C. perfossa	string o' buttons
C. pseudolycopodiodes	princess pine
C. rupestris	rosary vine
C. teres	rattlesnake tail
C. tetragona	miniature pine tree
Echeveria derenbergii	painted lady
E. elegans	Mexican snowball
E. pulvinata	chenille plant
Echinocereus	hedgehog cactus
Echinopsis multiplex	Easter-lily cactus
Euphorbia caput-medusae	Medusa's head
E. fulgens	scarlet plume
E. heterophylla	mole plant
E. lactea cristata	elkhorn
E. mammillaris	corncob cactus
E. mammillaris 'variegata'	Indian corncob
E. pulcherrima	poinsettia
E. tirucalli	pencil tree; milk bush
Faucaria tigrina	tiger jaws
Gasteria caespitosa	pencil leaf
Gymnocalycium mihanovichii	plain cactus
G. mihanovichii friedrichii	rose-plaid cactus red cap; Oriental moon
Hatiora salicornioides	drunkard's dream
Haworthia	
Hoya carnosa	wax plant
Kalanchoe daigremontiana	devil's backbone
K. pinnata (Bryophyllum)	air plant; miracle leaf
K. tomentosa	panda plant
Lithops	stoneface; cleft stone
Lobivia	
Mammillaria bocasana	powder puff
M. camptotricha	birdsnest
M. candida	snowball pincushion

sand is the obvious choice as a ground cover. Gravel chips and small sandstone pebbles are sometimes effective also. In addition, small pieces of driftwood may be used. Children in particular like to include figurines and other Lilliputian objects in a desertscape which may also tell a story of fact or fantasy.

If the walls of your container are transparent and fairly deep, consider adding more than the usual three layers of gravel, charcoal chips, and potting soil. You might work with different colored sands, for example, creating a painted-desert effect with different colors undulating and contrasting like a geological cross section of the earth.

With the possible exception of hoya and *Scilla violacea*, the cacti and other succulents listed on pages 64–65 are not suited to planting in moist, woodsy terrariums and bottle gardens. Ideas for using these plants in combination with animals are included in a discussion of Vivariums which may be found in the book *Miniature Gardens* by Elvin McDonald (Grosset & Dunlap).

The tall devil's backbone (Kalanchoe daigremontiana) appears like graceful palms above a desert oasis, in this dish garden.

Latin Name	Popular Name
M. elongata	golden stars
	lace cactus
M. fragilis	thimble cactus
M. hahniana	old lady cactus
M. lasiacantha	lace-spine cactus
M. plumosa	feather cactus
Monanthes	
Notocactus mammulosus	lemon ball
N. rutilans	pink ball cactus
N. scopa	silver ball
Opuntia basilaris	beaver tail
O. bigelovii	cholla cactus; teddy bear
O. clavarioides	black fingers
O. cylindrica	emerald idol
O. engelmannii	tuna
O. erectoclada	dominoes
O. erinacea ursina	grizzly bear
O. microdasys	bunny ears
O. microdasys albata	angora bunny ears
O. miscrodasys albispina	polka dots
O. microdasys 'Lutea'	honey Mike
O. oricola	prickly pear
O. rufida	cinnamon cactus
O. schickendantzii	lion's tongue
O. streptacantha	tuna cardona
O. strobiliformis	spruce cones
O. turpinii (glomerata)	paperspine cactus
O. vulgaris (monacantha)	Irish mittens
O. vulgaris variegata	Joseph's coat
x Pachyveria *	
Pelecyphora	jewel plant
	jeweled crown
Portulacaria afra	elephant bush
P. afra variegata	rainbow bush
Rebutia	
Rhipsalidopsis	
Rhipsalis cassutha	mistletoe cactus
R. warmingiana	popcorn cactus
Scilla violacea	silver squill
Sedum morganianum	burro tail
S. pachyphyllum	jelly beans
S. rubrotinctum	Christmas cheer
S. sieboldii	October plant
S. stahlii	coral beads
S. treleasei	silver sedum

* x indicates hybrid.

Snowy echeveria in a wok can be the table center-piece one moment and a terrace decoration the next.

A fantasy of cacti and succulents beside a permanent clump of cactus.

7
How to Multiply Cacti/Succulents

Plant propagation is a means of increasing not only your plants but also your enjoyment and involvement with them. The pleasure of nurturing a plant from seed, or the excitement of a successful graft, must be experienced to be appreciated. In addition to the satisfaction involved, making more plants from one offers the advantages of saving the cost of nursery-grown stock, or of obtaining a new plant from a rare one that may be difficult to acquire. And you can be sure that the plant you raise is the variety you want—ready-conditioned to your own particular climate.

Like other plants, cacti and succulents can be grown from seed, propagated by cuttings, or grafted one to another. Special techniques are involved with each, but cacti and succulents are more-than-willing parents, and with a little help a handful of plants can become an indoor or outdoor garden.

Seeds

If you don't mind the time involved, growing from seed is the best way to acquire a large number of plants at little expense. Seeds can be obtained from a nursery or harvested from your plants' seed pods. The best time for sowing seeds is spring or early summer, especially in temperate areas, so the seeds will have time to sprout before winter.

You will need a shallow container, and since drainage isn't crucial, almost anything handy will do. For large numbers of seeds, though, a nursery flat, a commercially available plastic seed flat, or a large, shallow box are recommended. You can divide these into compartments and sow different seeds at the same time. Be sure you label each or you'll lose track of what seeds are sown where.

Use vermiculite or a basic mix of equal parts peat moss and coarse sand. Don't pack the mix down, but allow it to fill the container rather loosely. Moisten the mix thoroughly and tip the container to empty it of any excess water. Place large seeds just below the soil surface by hand or with a pair of tweezers, and sprinkle tiny seeds, such as those of crassula, over the surface of the mix. Cover with a sheet of clear glass or plastic. Or you can use a piece of plastic food wrap.

Put the seed flat in a warm (78°F.), bright place, such as a window sill, but not in direct sunlight. Indoor plant lights, burning 14 to 16 hours out of every 24, are very good for germinating seeds. Keep testing the soil to be sure it is evenly moist. The enclosed container will hold moisture for long periods of time, and the seeds will probably not need watering more than once every two or three weeks. Always water with a fine mist or an eye dropper, so as not to disturb the delicate seeds. The germination period (the length of time required before the first sprouts appear) can vary from a few days (Stapeliads) to a year (some cactus species).

It will take a sharp eye to see the tiny seedlings, but when these are several months old and of manageable size, they need to be given plenty of light and air. Transplant them, several to a pot, and place, uncovered, in a sunny, well-ventilated location. When the containers become crowded, transplant individual plants into pots no larger than 2 inches. Larger pots hold moisture too long.

Cuttings, Divisions, and Offsets

The natural growth habit of cacti and succulents makes them well suited for propagation by cuttings, divisions, or offsets. Offsets are the little "baby" offshoots of new growth that form on the flower stalks of agaves, aloes, crassulas, and haworthias and at the bases of various other succulents. When a few inches in size, these may be pulled or cut off and rooted in their own containers.

Plants that form a dense mat of individual crowns, such as sempervivum, can be propagated by division. This means that the crowns can be pulled apart and replanted individually. Each crown, after separation from the others, retains its own root system, making it well on the way to being a self-sufficient plant.

Cuttings can be taken from either leaves or sections of stem that have leaf nodes. Good candidates for propagation by leaf cuttings are crassulas, kalanchoes, gasterias, and haworthias. Cut off either a whole leaf or a leaf section and mark it to remind you which end is up. Then set it aside for a few days to dry.

Plant one or many sections of leaf, bottom ends down, in light, sandy soil (three parts sand to one part loam). Don't push the leaves too deeply into the mix; they need only break the soil surface, and there will be enough contact for roots to form. Place in a warm, shaded location and keep the soil evenly moist. When the cuttings begin to look healthy or richer in color, you'll know that roots have formed. You can then dig up each leaf or leaf section and plant it in its own pot.

Whichever of these methods of propagation you choose, remember that the offspring will need warmth, even moisture and protection from direct sunlight until they have formed roots. Also, the best time of year for propagating is spring. At that time your plants are completely rested and ready for new growth.

Grafting

This technique is more a curiosity and a source of enjoyment for the adventuresome grower than it is a practical means of propagation, although it is sometimes the only way to get a stubborn plant to respond. Basically, grafting involves joining one plant to another

Flat graft (left) is best for rounded or globular scions; cleft (center) and side (right) grafts help make more slender scions succeed.

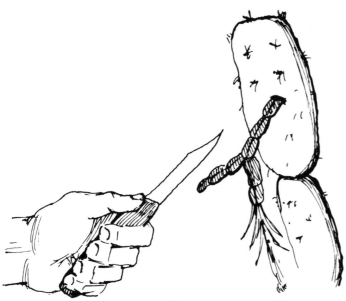

The stab graft is best for grafting trailing cactus species to fleshy stem cactus stock (opuntia, in this case). Make upward stab in stock and insert scion.

Until the graft takes, hold scion in place with rubber bands (as shown), toothpicks or long cactus spines.

with the hope that the host plant (understock) will support healthy growth in the guest plant (scion). And it is often the case that two grafted plants grow as one better than either would by itself. But in actuality, grafting of cacti is most often done to create even more bizarre and unusual shapes than already exist in this fascinating family of plants.

Only members of the cactus, euphorbia, and milkweed families can be grafted. These have in common what is called a cambium layer. This is the layer of growth that surrounds the plant, and the two plants to be joined must be matched at this point for the graft to succeed.

The four methods of grafting commonly used for succulents are: the flat graft, in which both the understock and the scion are cut straight across and joined; the cleft graft, in which a wedge-cut scion is fitted into a cleft-cut stock; the side graft, in which both stock and scion are cut at the same angle and joined; and the stab graft, in which a deep upward cut is made in the stock and the scion is wedged into it. Each method has its own advantages and works best with certain plant combinations. The flat graft is least difficult and is used especially for ball-shaped scions; the cleft and side grafts for tall, narrow stocks and scions; and the stab graft for flat, trailing plants.

The best time to graft is during the summer months when both stock and scion are in full, vigorous growth. It's especially important that you select healthy stock. Cut with a clean, sharp knife and join the pieces as quickly as possible. Be sure the cambium layers of both meet, and secure the scion in place with spines, rubber bands, or toothpicks. Once the graft takes, the spines will dissolve naturally, but toothpicks (which will leave slight scars) or rubber bands must be removed.

Before being joined, the stock and scion should be trimmed so that both parts fit as closely as possible. If too much sap runs from the cut surfaces, soak the pieces in water for a few minutes. This will dissolve the sap and make joining the pieces easier. Keep your newly grafted plants in shade for a few days and check rubber bands occasionally to be sure they are not too tight.

8
Positive Answers to the Negatives

If you buy only healthy, well-cultivated plants or seedlings from a reputable nursery, and care for them properly, they will be provided with a built-in resistance to disease and bothersome garden pests. Only neglected and poorly grown cacti and succulents suffer any real damage from the various ills and predators that threaten them. Preventive medicine is the best kind; it is far easier to build immunity with good soil, sun, and moisture than it is to eliminate infestation once it has taken over a plant. But there are safe and effective steps you can take if any of your plants falls prey to infection.

Pests

There are various bugs and almost microscopic animals that, given the chance, will enjoy chewing at or sucking the juices from cacti and succulents. Plants are especially susceptible indoors where these parasites have no natural enemies, and are therefore free to multiply and ravage as they please. Outdoors, ants are the principal problem because they act as temporary hosts to the insects that actually do the damage. Ants carry aphids and mealybugs from plant to plant, in return for which they eat these pests' secretions. Control ants in your garden and greenhouse with a good ant poison and you'll control dangerous pests. But never sprinkle ant powder or any of the other ant killers directly on your plants.

Aphids: These are tiny, greenish-colored insects that pierce the skin of cacti and succulents and suck out the juicy sap. They will cause twisted leaves and areas of discoloration on foliage. Flower buds and fruit will also be affected. To eliminate these pests, use malathion or spray with a nicotine sulfate–soap solution. You can make this yourself by adding one teaspoon mild soap flakes and one-half teaspoon Black Leaf 40 to one quart warm water. Water plants thoroughly the day before you intend to spray and wash off the residue a few hours after spraying.

Mealybugs: More difficult than aphids to kill, these sucking parasites are fuzzy white or gray insects about the size of a grain of wheat. They attack spines, stems, and roots of succulents, especially if the plant is overly dry. If you discover only a few, they can be picked off individually with tweezers. Or you can touch them with an alcohol-soaked cotton swab to kill them instantly. For heavier infestations, spray with malathion or the nicotine-soap solution. Mealybugs on large plants outdoors can often be knocked off with a strong jet of water from a hose.

Scale: The most stubborn of all pests to eradicate because of their hard outer shells, scale will look like pinhead-sized brown or whitish protuberances on stems and around the areoles on cacti. For minor infestations, dip a toothbrush in the nicotine-soap solution and scrub the infected areas. For more serious cases, use malathion according to the directions on the container.

Root-knot Nematodes: These are microscopic, wormlike animals that attack the roots of succulents, such as echeverias and euphorbias. They are evidenced by swellings along the roots and plants that turn pale in color and stop growing. Affected plants should be dug up, their roots pruned drastically and allowed to dry out for a few days. Plant in fresh soil, preferably sterilized. If you have any doubts about the soil, sterilize it by heating it in a 180-degree oven for an hour.

Thrips and Red Spiders: These tend to appear when plants are kept too dry and warm, especially indoors where ventilation is apt to be inadequate. The first signs are small yellow or white spots on stems or leaves. Fortunately, these mites are easily eradicated with malathion or the nicotine-soap solution.

Snails and Slugs: These chewing villains are the chief predators of cacti and succulents outdoors. Help keep your garden free of them by clearing weeds and thick brush, where they tend to breed. To kill them, scatter metaldehyde, a poisonous bait, on the soil around your plants. Beetles, grubs, and sow bugs are additional garden pests that can pose a threat to

cacti and succulents, and these chewers also can be eradicated with metaldehyde.

Diseases

Fungus infection is the chief disease a cactus or succulent plant is likely to develop. But again, like pests, it will attack only those plants that have been neglected or mistreated in some way. If a plant has been overwatered, underwatered, or has been bruised or cut and not cared for, it will be susceptible to the growth of fungus and the decay it causes.

When a fungus infection takes hold of it, a plant will droop and become discolored. To restore it to good health, it's necessary to find the point of infestation and cut out all of the decay until only healthy tissue remains. Then dust the open wound with sulfur or captan and allow it to dry out.

Another disease cacti and succulents sometimes develop is black rot, an infection that enters a plant through a break in its skin. Healthy tissue will turn into a soft, black mass, which eventually will spread throughout the plant. If caught in time, this disease can be dealt with in the same way as fungus infections.

Other Problems

In addition to pests and diseases, cacti and succulents that are poorly cared for are subject to various physiological disorders. Some of the symptoms appear to be the same as those caused by insects or fungus, but if you can find no evidence of these and your plant still shows signs of ill health, take stock of its growing conditions to be sure it's getting the air, light, heat, and moisture it needs.

For example, too much sun will cause foliage to develop yellow spots that will eventually turn brown and crusty. Frost-bitten plant tissues will turn soft to the touch, and if only small areas are affected, these should be cut away as soon as possible. Allow the rest of the plant to dry out and then resume normal culture. Succulents receiving too little air and light will develop abnormal growth that is long, rangy, and twisted. This phenomenon is called etiolation, and it can be corrected simply by supplying needed sun and ventilation.

If you keep in mind the fact that all of the afflictions described in this chapter are the result of negligence, and cultivate your plants with preventative care, then you'll never really have anything to worry about. Above all, don't become one of those gardening zealots who is constantly spraying and fertilizing unnecessarily. Chemical sprays are ultimately harmful to plants and should not be used unless you are certain your plants are infected. And stimulants, hormones, etc.—often used indiscriminately to compensate for otherwise inattentive cultivation or to satisfy impatience—are unnecessary. Don't succumb to the temptation of using them, but give your plants only what nature provides; it has done pretty well the past billion or so years and is difficult to improve upon. Finding out what nature wants for such varied groups of plants is up to you.

9
Nature's Curiosities

If you like to read science fiction, you will almost certainly want to grow some of the strange cacti and succulents illustrated in this chapter. Some are mere mimics—living stones and purple baby toes, for example. Others, like the elkhorn, mimic many strange and sculptured forms. The windowed succulents offer a study in the remarkable ability of plants to adapt to natural growing conditions. In the desert these curiosities have small, translucent areas at the ends of their stems that continue to admit needed sunlight even though the rest of the plant may become covered with sand.

If far-out plants appeal to you, consider one of the globes that sends out strange tentaclelike growths, or an old man cactus covered with silky, long white hairs. There are some cacti and succulents that have irregularly flattened or fasciated growth that you may find appealing—or a monstrosity. In fact, the Latin word *monstrosus* appears frequently in listings of cacti and succulents.

A monstrose plant forms multiple shoots of irregular growth from its growing tip. A fasciated or cristate plant is one that has developed twisted, snakelike growth, that can take different forms among botanically identical plants. Scientists still argue about the causes of these oddities; they've been attributed to damage or disease, excessive or inadequate feeding, or environmental conditions. Whatever, they're sought after by many growers to the extent that they become avid collectors of nothing else. It is, of course, a matter of personal taste, but a few of these tend to go a long way in a plant collection. Each is like a piece of living sculpture. Select with care, then give each a container uniquely suited to showing it off. Although you may cultivate the plants wherever you can give them the best care, from time to time bring each one to a living area where it can be lighted dramatically and properly appreciated by you and your friends.

All the bizarre plants illustrated in this chapter are available commercially in this country, either from local specialists or by mail from one of the growers listed in the Appendix. But some are rare indeed, so rare that importers and growers will exchange single specimens like rare coins. True aficionados will only lend their best-loved plants just as museums or galleries lend their most-desired paintings.

Senecio fulgens—*scarlet kleinia*.

Euphorbia ornithopus.

Lobivia densispina *crest—lily cactus*.

Dorstenia hildebrantii.

Bowiea volubilis—*climbing onion.*

Gerrardanthus macrorhizus.

Cotyledon reticulata.

Senecio pendulus—*green marble vine.*

Othonna herrei.

Frithia pulchra—*purple baby toes.*

Melocactus violaceus—*Turk's cap.*

Gibbaeum album—*flowering quartz.*

Thrixanthocereus blossfeldiorum.

Sarcocaulon herrei.

Appendixes

Locally look for cacti and other succulents wherever plants are sold. Before you buy, check for any signs of insect pests, rot near the soil line, or mechanical damage. Plants found at supermarkets and dimestores are often incorrectly labeled—if at all. You'll enjoy any plant more if you know its correct name, and you'll also be able to better care for it.

Unless a specialist in cacti and other succulents lives close enough for you to visit, the best way to assemble a collection is to order by mail. Favorite sources are included in the list that follows.

Cacti/Succulents Sources by Mail

Abbey Garden, Box 30331, Santa Barbara, Calif. 93105—Complete listing of cacti and other succulents; catalog 25¢.

Cactus Gem Nursery, 10092 Mann Dr., Cupertino, Calif. (visit Thurs.-Sun.); by mail write P.O. Box 327, Aromas, Calif. 95004.

Davis Cactus Garden, 1522 Jefferson St., Kerrville, Tex. 78028—Send 25¢ for catalog.

Fernwood Plants, 1311 Fernwood Pacific Dr., Topanga, Calif. 90290—Rare and unusual cacti.

Grigsby Cactus Gardens, 2354 Bella Vista Dr., Vista, Calif. 92083—Catalog 50¢.

Helen's Cactus, 2205 Mirasol, Brownsville, Tex. 78520—Send stamp for list.

Henrietta's Nursery, 1345 N. Brawley Ave., Fresno, Calif. 93705—Cacti/succulents; catalog 20¢.

Kirkpatrick's, 27785 De Anza St., Barstow, Calif. 92311—Cacti/succulents; send 10¢ stamp for list.

Modlin's Cactus Gardens, Rt. 4, Box 3034, Vista, Calif. 92083—Catalog 25¢.

Cactus by Mueller, 10411 Rosedale Highway, Bakersfield, Calif. 93308—10¢ stamp for list.

Smith's Cactus Garden, P.O. Box 871, Paramount, Calif. 90723—Send 30¢ for list.

Ed Storms, 4223 Pershing, Ft. Worth, Tex. 76107—Lithops and other succulents.

H. E. Wise, 3710 June St., San Bernardino, Calif. 92405—Cacti; send stamp for list.

Specialists in Artificial Light for Plants *

Aladdin Industries, Inc., Nashville, Tenn. 37210—Manufacturers of growth chambers and fluorescent-light gardening equipment.

* NOTE: *Ordinary and special agricultural fluorescents and incandescents made by such firms as General Electric, Sylvania, Westinghouse, and Durotest are stocked by the firms listed here, excepting Verilux, which sells only the TruBloom. Many of the bulbs as well as fixtures are also available at local electrical supply houses.*

Fleco Industries, 3347 Halifax St., Dallas, Tex. 75247—Attractive fluorescent-lighted shelves for plants.

Floralite Co., 4124 E. Oakwood Rd., Oak Creek, Wis. 53154—Fluorescent-light gardening equipment and supplies.

The Greenhouse, 9515 Flower St., Bellflower, Calif. 90706—Fluorescent-light gardening equipment.

Indoor Gardening Supplies, P.O. Box 40551, Detroit, Mich. 48240—Fluorescent-light gardening equipment.

J & D Lamps, 245 S. Broadway, Yonkers, N.Y. 10705—Fluorescent-light gardening equipment.

Shoplite Co., Inc., 566 Franklin Ave., Nutley, N.J. 07110—Fluorescent-light gardening equipment; catalog 25¢.

Tube Craft, Inc., 1311 W. 80th St., Cleveland, Ohio 44102—Fluorescent-light gardening equipment.

Verilux TruBloom, 35 Mason St., Greenwich, Conn. 06830—Manufacturers of TruBloom fluorescents for plants.

Societies to Join

Cactus and Succulent Society of America, Inc., 1593 Las Canoas Road, Santa Barbara, Calif. 93105. Members receive the excellent bimonthly magazine called the Cactus and Succulent Journal.

Indoor Light Gardening Society of America, 128 West 58th Street, New York, N.Y. 10019.

Important Cacti/Succulents Collections to Visit

Arizona: Boyce Thompson Southwestern Arboretum, Superior. Desert Botanical Garden, Phoenix.

California: Huntington Gardens, San Marino. Lotusland (estate of Mme Ganna Walska), by appointment only, Santa Barbara. Rancho Santa Ana Botanic Garden, Claremont. University of California Botanical Garden, Berkeley.

Hawaii: Pa'u-a-Laka Gardens, Koloa, Poipu, Kauai.

Michigan: University of Michigan, Ann Arbor.

Missouri: Missouri Botanical Garden, St. Louis.

New York: Brooklyn Botanic Garden, Brooklyn. New York Botanical Garden, Bronx Park.

Pennsylvania: Longwood Gardens, Kennett Square.

Canada: Montreal Botanical Garden, Montreal.

Index